CULTURALLY SPEAKING

A Conversation and Culture Text for Learners of English

Rhona B. Genzel

Martha Graves Cummings

Rochester Institute of Technology
Learning Development Center

1817

HARPER & ROW, PUBLISHERS, New York
Cambridge, Philadelphia, San Francisco, London, Mexico City,
São Paulo, Singapore, Sydney

PHOTO CREDITS

Antman, Stock, Boston: Page 85 (top right)
Greg Bertolini: Pages 2, 3 (middle, bottom right), 7, 8, 12 (left)
Martha Graves Cummings: Pages 3 (bottom left), 10, 45 (middle),
    46, 77, 78 (top), 85 (bottom left and right), 97, 125, 142
Bill Gage: Pages 3 (top), 11, 12 (right), 143
Herwig, Stock, Boston: Page 78 (bottom)
Powers, Stock, Boston: Page 85 (top left)
H. Armstrong Roberts: Page 86
Nancy M. Stuart: Pages 9, 45 (right)
Cornelia Van Der Linde: Page 45 (left)

Sponsoring Editor: Robert Miller
Project Editor: Brigitte Pelner
Text Design: Leon Bolognese
Cover Design: Miriam Recio
Text Art: Steven Duquette (cartoons); Mario Ferro (puzzles)
Photo Research: Mira Schachne
Production: Jeanie Berke/Delia Tedoff
Compositor: York Graphic Services
Printer and Binder: The Murray Printing Company

Culturally Speaking: A Conversation and Culture Text for Learners of English

Library of Congress Cataloging in Publication Data

Genzel, Rhona B.
    Culturally speaking.

    Includes index.
    1. English language—Textbooks for foreign speakers. 2. English language—Conversation and phrase books. 3. Simulation games in education.
I. Cummings, Martha Graves. II. Title.
PE1128.G37   1986   428.3'4   85-21983
ISBN 0-06-042292-0

85 86 87 88 9 8 7 6 5 4 3 2 1

Since culture is the continuation of traditions and customs from one generation to the next, we would like to dedicate this book to

Our grandparents   Bertha and Jacob Beldegreen
Lawrence Jackson

Our parents   Raymond and Gertrude Beldegreen
John and Anna Lee Graves

Our husbands   George Genzel
Ralph Cummings

Our children   Robert and Brette Genzel
Jennifer Schaefer and Aimee Francesca Cummings
David Cummings
Lisa Schaefer

And   Vincent McGuire, who passed on the
tradition of teaching

contents

Appendix: Simulation Game Directions 154

overview

Culturally Speaking is a conversation textbook that focuses on the importance that cultural elements play in communication. The text is designed to develop conversational fluency in a variety of situations. *Culturally Speaking* has been developed for use with intermediate and advanced ESL students and may be used in high school, college, adult education, or industrial training programs. This book has been designed for people who are new to the United States or who plan to live, work, or travel in the U.S.A.

Culturally Speaking is based on the concepts that people learn most effectively through doing and that communication involves knowledge not only of the language but also of the culture. Throughout the book, students make and share cross-cultural comparisons and practice conversations in realistic, everyday situations as they learn about American customs and culture. Rather than experiencing English in isolation, students experience language in its natural context, replete with gestures and social amenities needed for effective communication. Students learn how to interact comfortably with native speakers, on the telephone, at social gatherings, and in educational situations. They learn to make introductions and small talk, participate in an American classroom by asking and responding to questions, explain medical problems to a doctor, and go shopping in a department store. In addition, students discover how to respond to invitations and to deal with friends in times of happiness and difficulty.

As students work through the Quick Customs Quizzes and Let's Share exercises, they are reminded that people around the world have different values and customs. The text makes no attempt to pass judgment but serves as a vehicle for learning about others as it encourages interest in and respect for other cultures while teaching conversation.

to the teacher

The goal of *Culturally Speaking* is to get students talking and acting comfortably in a variety of situations. To do this, each chapter focuses on a different aspect of mainstream American culture. Students begin by making cultural comparisons and sharing information about their culture; they move on to model conversations, half dialogues, role plays, and ultimately simulation games. As students complete each chapter, they become more and more proficient, not only in the language but also in the cultural context in which language is used. They become proficient with a variety of situations and self-confident about their ability to communicate.

To accomplish this, each chapter contains a variety of creative exercises to spark student interest in culture and to provide them with the conversational and cultural tools they need to communicate effectively. Some of the activities included in the book and suggested methods of use are listed here.

LET'S SHARE

Let's Share is designed to encourage discussion on a topic that students are uniquely qualified to discuss—their country and its customs. Students enjoy this exercise because they know the content well and are eager to share information about their culture with others. Therefore, in addition to teaching cultural elements, it fosters lively discussions. In this exercise, after the students have filled in the comparison charts, they should be encouraged to share that information with members of the class. The atmosphere should be one of genuine interest and curiosity. No judgments should be permitted on the merits of one culture over another. Each should be accepted at face value and appreciated for its uniqueness. This sharing creates an atmosphere of mutual respect and openness.

Teachers may encourage students to bring in photographs or pictures from magazines depicting the elements of culture being discussed.

MODEL DIALOGUES

Before students are asked to provide dialogue or to converse, they are provided with model conversations. The conversations should be practiced orally with appropriate body language and gestures.

1. Students should discuss what body language would be appropriate for each person in the dialogue. (Students may refer to "Gestures and Body Language" in Chapter One.)
2. Once the body language has been established, students may be asked to act out the model dialogues using appropriate gestures.
3. In more advanced classes, students may be asked if there is other body language that could be used. They may then act out the dialogue using alternative body language. The class can then discuss if the body language changed the meaning of the dialogue.
4. Students may enact the dialogues in different ways:

   a. Have two students enact the dialogue while laughing.
   b. Have two students enact the dialogue very seriously.
   c. Have them enact the dialogue not looking at each other.

   Discuss how each approach changes the meaning of the words.

NOW YOU DO IT

Once students have completed the cultural sharing, practiced the idioms and phrases, and manipulated the model dialogues, they are ready to prepare responses to half dialogues. This is the next step from sample dialogues and leads to free conversations, role plays, and ultimately simulation games.

1. Students may work in small groups or pairs to complete the half dialogues.
2. More advanced students may write an original conversation.
3. Once the dialogues have been written:

   a. Students may be asked to take turns practicing them.
   b. Students may be asked to discuss appropriate facial and hand gestures for each person in the dialogue.
   c. Two students should then be asked to act them out, with appropriate gestures, in front of the class.
   d. If several tape recorders are available, students in each group can tape their dialogues. These tapes may then be played back for the students to hear how they sound.
   e. The instructor may wish to tape or videotape some of the conversations. These can then be written on the chalkboard for the teacher to point out grammatical elements and idiomatic usage. The videotape may be used to discuss the facial and hand gestures as well as language elements.
   f. Students may practice the dialogues with the tapes that accompany *Culturally Speaking*.

ROLE PLAY

In role play, the students are given a situation and must respond spontaneously. Role play comes closest to natural conversation because the participants in the role play do not know in advance what their partner is going to say.

1. Students may work in pairs enacting situations while the teacher circulates, listens to the conversation, and provides assistance when necessary.
2. Several conversations may be taped, transcribed onto the chalkboard, and discussed in terms of grammatical forms and appropriate idiom usage.
3. To improve listening comprehension, the class may be divided into groups. Two students converse while a third listens and writes down observations.

Many options are available to the teacher to vary the use of the Let's Share section. We suggest the following options:

1. The first time the Let's Share section is used, the teacher may want to lead the discussion with the class as a whole. This way the teacher can establish a tone of mutual respect and appreciation.
2. Students may be asked to work in groups of three or four. One student in each group should be assigned the task of reporting to the class what the group has discussed.
3. Students may be organized in pairs. One student is assigned the role of speaker and for five minutes must discuss his or her culture in terms of the information on the Let's Share page. The other student is assigned the responsibility of listening carefully. The listener should not take notes. When the speaker has finished talking, the listener must repeat what he or she has heard. The speaker then indicates if the listener has reported the information correctly. The students then change roles: The person who was the listener now becomes the speaker and talks about his or her culture. The person who was the speaker becomes the listener. This is an excellent way to increase listening comprehension and is a good device to make sure that the listener is, in fact, paying attention.

ANALYSIS

Analysis sections are closely related to Let's Share sections. As students analyze how people in other countries do or perceive things and make comparisons with their own culture, they arrive at a deeper understanding of themselves and of others. The information provided in these sections becomes the basis for later communication practice.

QUICK CUSTOMS QUIZ

The Quick Customs Quiz is a fast-paced exercise in which students read situations and choose the answer they feel is the most appropriate way to deal with the situation. Answers at the end of the book reflect how a mainstream American would respond in a similar situation. Students may be asked to choose answers as they think an American would or to choose as they would for their culture. Discussion of the answers should then follow.

One approach to the Quick Customs Quiz is for students to complete the exercise for homework and come to class prepared to discuss their answers. During in-class discussion, cross-cultural comparisons can be made. Students should be encouraged to discuss how they feel about dealing with situations in the way the book suggests a mainstream American would act. The instructor may also discuss alternate methods of handling situations.

VOCABULARY, IDIOMS, AND PHRASES

Some situations require knowledge of special terminology. Therefore, key vocabulary words and expressions such as those used when dating, eating out, going to the doctor, making introductions, responding to invitations, and using the telephone are provided. Students learn the terms in a conversational context and may use them in a variety of ways:

1. Through oral reading and conversation.
2. By asking students to use the terms in sentences on their own. These sentences should then be rewritten, substituting a blank for the expression. Students should then exchange papers and fill in the appropriate expression in the blank spaces.

SIMULATION GAMES

One of the unique features of *Culturally Speaking* is the integration of four simulation games into the text. Each game is used as the climax to the activities of a particular chapter. It is the simulation game that bridges the gap between using practical language in directed activities on a one-dimensional level and performing, interacting, responding, and initiating on a three-dimensional level that approximates the real world.

After students have practiced model dialogues, learned appropriate vocabulary and idioms, and completed conversations and role plays, they are ready to experience interaction as it occurs in the real world. The games, which focus on attending school, going out socially, shopping in a clothing store, and visiting the doctor, simulate activities students may encounter and provide them with an opportunity to interact in English.

The games are relatively easy to administer. The four games are briefly discussed here. For more information about running and setting up the games, see the Appendix and the setup and prop guide with each game.

1. *Attending School* (Chapter Two). Students ask the teacher questions, answer questions, and converse socially with other students. They practice being active participants in the classroom and use the language and culture supplied in the chapter to make appointments with teachers, ask appropriate questions, and engage in small talk with their classmates.
2. *Going to a Nightclub* (Chapter Six). Students must order from a menu, observe proper restaurant etiquette, make introductions, and interact

socially. They have the opportunity to use the language and social amenities they learned in the chapter on building friendships.

3. *Shopping in the United States* (Chapter Seven). Students buy goods, ask about sizes, make returns, and pay with cash, check, or credit card. This game is designed to give students practice using size charts and interacting with salespeople.

4. *Going to the Doctor* (Chapter Nine). Students go through all the general procedures for an office visit to the doctor. They must speak to the receptionist, fill out a health form, and talk with the doctor and nurse. Students practice terminology and procedures they learned in the chapter, which focus on a visit to the doctor's office.

ANSWERS

Answers to the exercises are provided in a separate section at the end of the book. Sometimes cultural elements are elaborated on to provide students with a better understanding of the concepts presented.

GLOSSARY

The glossary at the end of the book provides definitions for the difficult words and idioms used in the text. It also gives their part of speech and uses each item in a sentence so that students may see each word used in an appropriate context.

acknowledgments

Teachers are constantly learning and growing as they try new ideas and share their successes and failures with one another. No acknowledgment would be complete without thanking both the many teachers who, over the years, have shared their ideas with us and the students who have reacted to the new methods we presented and shared information about their cultures and language needs.

Special acknowledgment, however, goes to Jo Cone, who read the manuscript with a critical eye and always supported our efforts; Eva Yervasi, who piloted the material in conversation classes and offered suggestions; and Kathryn Bonnez, who piloted various sections and provided insightful comments. We would also like to thank Paul Ventura, who analyzed the photographs from a cross-cultural perspective. Finally, Martha Cummings would like to thank the late scholar T. Walter Herbert and Roseanna Prater, who taught her to think creatively.

We would like to thank the following reviewers: Marjorie Vai; Priscilla Karant, The American Language Institute, New York University; John C. Homan, Florida International University; Janet Ross, Ball State University; William W. Jex, The American Language Institute, New York University; Julie Weissman, Triton College; and Marilyn Rosenthal, Syntactix International.

We would also like to thank Bill Gage, our colleague and friend; Greg Bertolini; and all the people who posed for the photographs.

Rhona B. Genzel
Martha Graves Cummings

Getting Along with People

Each of us from different cultural backgrounds has a unique way of doing things, analyzing situations, and reacting to circumstances. Our individual way of viewing a situation is called *perception*.

Look at the pictures below. What do you see?

Depending on your perception, you will see either a vase or the profile of two faces in figure A. In figure B, depending on your perception, you will see either an old woman or a young woman. See p. 159 for solution.

Just as our perception of lines in black and white can be changed, so can our perceptions of life. This difference in perceptions makes up cultures.

To live comfortably in another country, you need to understand its thinking and expectations. In *Culturally Speaking*, you will experience how people in the United States think, live, and act. You will also see how Americans perceive others and interpret actions and behaviors. At the same time, you will compare your own culture, traditions, and ways of responding to situa-

tions and share them with your classmates. As you share your knowledge and learn from others, you will not only learn English but also begin to understand life in the United States.

1 HAND GESTURES

Even before people begin to talk, you can tell a great deal about them by observing their gestures. Gestures can tell about the person's attitudes, feelings, and interests.

LET'S SHARE

Gestures may have more than one meaning. In fact, they may mean something totally different from one culture to the next. Look at the photograph below and those on page 3.

In the United States, this gesture symbolizes victory or triumph. In the Soviet Union, it signifies friendship.

This gesture in the United States means that something is good, acceptable, or "OK." However, in parts of South America, it may be interpreted to have a vulgar meaning.

MATCHING

Below are some commonly used hand gestures. Match each picture with its meaning in the United States. Check your answers on page 159.

1.

2.

3.

4.

5.

A. _____ To show that you have won

B. _____ To ask someone to come closer to you

C. _____ To wish for good luck

D. _____ To ask someone to stop

E. _____ To show approval

3

LET'S SHARE

Look at the pictures on pages 2 and 3. Do any of these gestures have a different meaning in your country? Indicate the letter of the gesture in the gesture column in the chart on page 5. Then explain how it is used in your country.

HAND-GESTURE IDIOMS

The English language is rich in *idioms*. Here are some commonly used idioms that involve the hands. Try to match the idiom with its meaning. Check your answers on page 159.

_____ 1. To be empty-handed

A. To be bored; to have nothing to do

_____ 2. At one's fingertips

B. To steal

_____ 3. To have a finger in the pie

C. To be clumsy

_____ 4. To have sticky fingers

D. Completely under another person's control

_____ 5. To have butterfingers

E. To attempt to do something

_____ 6. To have something in hand

F. Easily available

_____ 7. Wrapped around someone's finger

G. To be involved in something

_____ 8. To twiddle one's thumbs

H. To have something under control

_____ 9. To try one's hand at something

I. To lack something that is needed

ROLE PLAY

Below is a list of situations in which you can use hand gestures to show how you feel. Choose one situation and act it out in front of the class. The object of this exercise is for your classmates to guess which situation you have chosen by watching your gestures.

1. You want someone to come to you.
2. You want to show approval.
3. You want to show that your team has just won the game.
4. You want to wish someone good luck.
5. You want someone to stop coming toward you.

Gesture	What It Means	When You Would Use It
1.		
2.		
3.		

2 NONVERBAL CUES

Nonverbal cues are gestures we use to let other people know what we think, want, or feel without using words. These gestures or nonverbal cues are used in many ways. The chart below gives several nonverbal cues and their uses. In the space provided, explain what nonverbal cues are used in your culture in the same situations.

Purpose	*Nonverbal Cue in the United States*	*Nonverbal Cue in Your Country*
1. To get the waiter's attention	Raise your hand.	
2. To ask the teacher a question	Raise your hand.	
3. To indicate you have to leave	Look at your watch, stand up, or begin to organize your belongings.	
4. To show someone something	Point using your index finger.	
5. To indicate *no*	Move your head from side to side.	
6. To indicate *yes*	Move your head up and down.	
7. To show you don't know something	Shrug your shoulders	

Box continued on following page

Purpose	Nonverbal Cue in the United States	Nonverbal Cue in Your Country
8. To share a secret or a joke	Wink.	

QUICK CUSTOMS QUIZ

Below are situations in which you might find yourself in the United States. Read each situation, decide what is appropriate, and choose the answer that best fits the circumstances. Draw a circle around the letter in front of your answer. Check your answers against those on page 159, which are the answers an American would probably give.

1. What emotion is this woman feeling, as shown by her smile and her open arms with clenched fists?

    a. Excitement
    b. Anger
    c. Confusion
    d. Disappointment

2. What does this gesture mean?

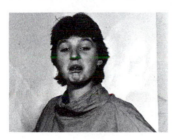

    a. Mockery
    b. Rebellion
    c. Contempt

3. If you ask someone a question and she replies in this way, what is she trying to tell you?

    a. Ask your question again.
    b. I don't know.
    c. I don't care.

4. If you see a person using this gesture, what is he doing?

   a. Getting angry
   b. Becoming bored
   c. Thinking

5. If you see someone talking and suddenly she reacts in this way, what is she?

   a. Surprised
   b. Interested in what someone across the room is talking about
   c. Angry

GESTURE IDIOMS

Here are some commonly used idioms that are based on nonverbal cues. Match the idiom with its meaning. Check your answers on page 160.

___ 1. With open arms	A. An irritation
___ 2. A pain in the neck	B. To disregard something
___ 3. To rub elbows with	C. To be involved in a project that is too difficult
___ 4. To keep a straight face	D. To socialize with
___ 5. To put your heads together	E. To act casually; to be oneself
___ 6. To be all ears	F. To listen attentively
___ 7. To shrug something off	G. To work together with someone; to share information
___ 8. To be in over one's head	H. Not to show one's true feelings; not to laugh under most circumstances

8

_____ 9. To let one's hair down

I. To work very hard

_____ 10. To go behind someone's back

J. To be dishonest; to do something without someone's knowledge or permission

_____ 11. To keep one's nose out of someone's business

K. To pay attention to only one's own concerns

_____ 12. To keep one's nose to the grindstone

L. In a welcoming and enthusiastic manner

NOW YOU DO IT

Form groups of three. As a group, decide on a situation you could act out using the gestures and nonverbal cues we have discussed so far. Rehearse your pantomime of the situation carefully. Make sure that your meaning is clear. Then act out the situation for the class. Ask them to tell you what happened and what gestures you used to get your points across.

BODY LANGUAGE

Whether they are aware of it or not, all people use *body language*. Body language is a combination of hand gestures, body movements, and facial expressions that people use when they speak. You will be amazed at the amount of information you can gather by just observing the people in the following photographs.

Photo Analysis

Look at each photograph. Answer the questions, and be prepared to share your answers. Also tell how a person from your culture would interpret the body language. Check your answers on page 160.

1. How well do these women know each other? How can you tell?

9

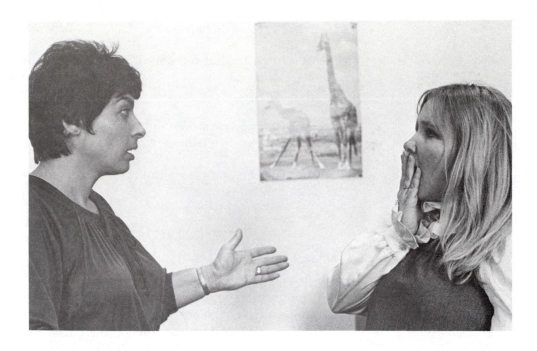

2. Who is talking? Who is surprised or shocked? Who is explaining? How can you tell?

3. Who is talking? How do you know? Are the listeners interested in what the speaker has to say? How do you know?

4. Look at the pictures on the following page. What is happening in each picture? How well do the people know each other? How does each person feel about what is being said? List the gestures and body language as you answer these questions. After you have finished, write a dialogue to go along with the sequence of photographs.

10

A.

B.

C.

Photo	Gestures	Meanings
A		

Box continued on following page

Box continued from preceding page

Photo	Gestures	Meanings
B		
C		

3 DISTANCE AND SPACE REQUIREMENTS

SPACE REQUIREMENTS

People from different cultures have different space requirements. For example, South Americans and Middle Easterners stand closer when they talk or sit together than North Americans or Asians.

In the United States, people need to have greater distances between them physically than people in many other cultures. Although Americans are often more affectionate and more likely to touch people they know, they have a great need for privacy, especially in the presence of strangers. For example, when Americans enter a bus, doctor's office, or waiting room, they sit at least one chair away from the nearest person if possible. Conversation distance with superiors or those they don't know well is about 3 to 4 feet.* However, intimate conversations may be held as close as 1½ feet apart. Because Americans feel uncomfortable if someone stands closer, they will instinctively move away. Should this happen, don't be offended. Your listener is merely stepping back to his or her normal conversational distance.

*Note that 12 inches = 1 foot; 1 inch = 2.54 centimeters; 1 centimeter = .394 inches.

Analysis

Other countries do not have the same "rules" for deciding how close to each other people sit or stand in different situations. Fill in the chart below for your country. The first situation has been filled in for the United States. When you have completed the chart, compare your answers with those on page 160, which are the answers an American would give.

Situation	Distance People Sit or Stand from Each Other	Type of Body Language People Use
1. Riding on a bus with people you don't know	People try to sit at least one seat from another person and avoid touching. They stand as far apart as possible.	Looking away or out the window, reading, crossing arms, clutching packages
2. Waiting in a doctor's office		
3. Waiting in line		
4. Eating lunch in a restaurant or café		
5. Talking to one's boss or teacher		
6. Talking to friends in a group		
7. Talking to a friend about something personal		

Box continued on following page

Situation	Distance People Sit or Stand from Each Other	Type of Body Language People Use
8. Talking to a stranger		
9. Talking to a child		

LET'S SHARE

Answer these questions about your own country to come up with a set of rules about distance in your culture. Then demonstrate the appropriate distance.

1. You wish to carry on a conversation with a person you don't know well. How far apart should you stand from this person? _____
2. You wish to talk intimately with someone you know well. How far apart should you be? _____
3. You are talking to a supervisor or an elder (your employer, a teacher, a clergyman, a government official). How far away should you stand? _____
4. When you enter a bus, a restaurant, a doctor's office, or any waiting room, how close should you sit to the nearest person? _____

4 INTRODUCTIONS

Everyone wants to meet people and make friends. A smile, a friendly look, or an open gesture indicates a person's interest in you. To introduce yourself, approach the individual, smile, and say, "Hello, my name is _____." Then shake hands with your friend by firmly taking his or her right hand in yours and pressing it gently but firmly.

MODEL DIALOGUES

ROBERT: Mr. Caldwell, I'd like you to meet my mother.

MR. CALDWELL: Mrs. Rienzo, I'm pleased to meet you.

MRS. RIENZO: Robert enjoys your class very much.

MR. CALDWELL: Thank you. I enjoy having him in class.

MRS. RIENZO: It was very nice meeting you.

MR. CALDWELL: Same here. Good-bye.

Introductions among young people or casual acquaintances are less formal. For example, an 8- or 9-year-old child would probably say, "Mom, this is my friend Peter." It is important to know that Americans, especially men, do not embrace unless they are very good friends who have not seen each other for a long time.

Here are some more model dialogues.

Introducing two friends:

TIM: John, I'd like you to meet my friend, Joan Sullivan. Joan, this is John Tracy.

JOAN: (*shaking hands with John*) It's nice to meet you.

Introducing your friend to your mother:

TIM: Phyllis, I'd like you to meet my mother, Mrs. Abrams. Mom, this is Phyllis Akerly.

PHYLLIS: I'm glad to meet you, Mrs. Abrams.

MRS. ABRAMS: I'm happy to meet you, too. Tim has talked so much about you.

Here are some more sample introductions. Notice that the person doing the introduction provides a little information about the person he or she is introducing. This often helps to start conversation between the people who are being introduced.

TOM: Mr. O'Malley, I'd like you to meet my friend, Maria Carlos. She is an exchange student from Spain and is majoring in computer science.

MR. O'MALLEY: I'm glad to meet you. I hope you've been able to get the courses you want. Computer science is such a popular major.

MARIA: Yes, thank you, I have. Fortunately, there are many courses I can choose from.

MR. O'MALLEY: That's good.

MARIA: Well, I have to go to class now. I certainly enjoyed meeting you.

MR. O'MALLEY: I hope we'll meet again. Good-bye.

MARIA: Good-bye.

JAMES: (*at a party where he doesn't know anyone*) Hello, my name is James Jones.

ANNA: Hi. I'm Anna Wells. It's nice to meet you.

JAMES: Do you know many people here? I don't know a single person!

ANNA: Really? Let me introduce you to some of my friends. James Jones, I'd like you to meet Mary Kempe. She goes to East High School and is a real sports enthusiast.

JAMES: Nice to meet you. What sports are you interested in?

MARY: My biggest interests are running and jogging. I try to run at least three miles a day. . . .

LET'S SHARE

Here is a chart that outlines how Americans greet each other. Compare these customs with customs in your country. Describe or demonstrate the body language you would use in your country.

Action	*In the United States*	*In Your Country*
1. Who makes the introduction?	Either the person who wishes to meet another or a friend who knows the other person.	
2. Who should be introduced to whom?	A woman to a man; a younger person to an older person; a subordinate to a superior.	
3. What should you say?	"Hello, my name is _____." "Mary Smith, I'd like you to meet my friend, John Jones." "Dr. Raman, this is my associate, Professor Allen." "Mrs. Buckett, I'd like to introduce my daughter, Jennifer."	
4. May a man introduce himself to a woman? May a woman introduce herself to a man?	Yes; yes.	
5. What body language should a person use (facial expressions, gestures)?	Smile, face the person, and look attentively at the person's eyes.	

Box continued on following page

Box continued from preceding page

Action	In the United States	In Your Country
6. What tone of voice should one use?	Quiet, but friendly.	
7. Does one shake hands when meeting someone? How should you shake hands?	Men always shake hands; if a woman extends her hand, shaking is appropriate. Firmly but gently.	
8. Do people embrace or kiss people of the same sex upon meeting? Does one kiss or hug children when one is introduced?	No, unless the people are very close friends. Men never kiss each other unless they are relations or very close friends. No.	

NOW YOU DO IT

Now that we have discussed introductions, it's time for you to do it. Be sure to incorporate the appropriate facial expressions, body language, and distance when talking.

The following conversation is appropriate at work, in school, in your neighborhood, or in any place where the same people usually see each other and would recognize you as being new.

STRANGER: Hi. You're new here, aren't you?

YOU: _____

STRANGER: My name is Barbara Levinson.

YOU: Will you say that again, please?

STRANGER: Yes, my name is Barbara Levinson. What is your name?

YOU: _____

STRANGER: How do you spell that?

YOU: _____

STRANGER: I'm really glad to meet you.

YOU: _____

As you can see from this dialogue, it is perfectly acceptable to ask someone to speak more slowly or to repeat what he or she has said. The other person will be pleased that you want to understand and are willing to ask questions.

5 SMALL TALK

After the introduction, people usually talk about topics of general interest, such as the weather, local events, work, or school. Topics of general interest are called *small talk*. They can be discussed easily without knowing the other person well. They are very good conversation starters.

Sometimes small talk is a way to meet someone or start a conversation.

In a classroom:

YOU: Hello, aren't you in my English class?

OTHER PERSON: Yes, I thought I'd seen you there before.

YOU: Did you finish the essay?

OTHER PERSON: No, I had trouble organizing my thoughts.

At a dance:

YOU: Excuse me. Do you know when the band is going to start playing?

OTHER PERSON: I believe they're going to start playing at nine-thirty.

YOU: Have they recorded any songs yet? I don't think I've ever heard of them before.

OTHER PERSON: I don't think so, but they're supposed to be really good.

Model Dialogues

Here are some examples of small talk.

1. PERSON A: Hi.
   PERSON B: Hello.
   A: It's a nice day, isn't it?
   B: Yes, and the weather is going to be warm all week. . . .

2. A: Did you see the paper this morning?
   B: No, why?
   A: There was a terrible accident on the road into town!
   B: Really, what happened? . . .

3. A: Did you see the football game on television last night?
   B: No, who was playing?
   A: The Green Bay Packers and the Detroit Tigers.
   B: What was the score? . . .

4. A: When is it going to stop snowing?
   B: The weatherman predicted snow until evening.
   A: Oh no, really?
   B: Yes, and another storm is moving in! . . .

CONVERSATION TOPICS

After you have introduced yourself, what should you talk about? What are some good things to talk about with your new friend? There are many choices, including the following:

1. The country you or the other person is from (What is it like? How does it compare to the United States?)
2. What the other person is studying or has studied in school (What are you studying in school? What is your favorite subject? What do you want to do after you graduate?)
3. The work that the other person does (What kind of work do you do? Do you like it? What do you enjoy about it? How did you decide to go into teaching, programing, painting, electronics, etc?)
4. The United States (What do you like about the United States? What interesting things have happened since you came here? How does this compare to your country?)
5. One's family
6. Current events

There are, however, some subjects that you should not talk about, especially with someone you don't know well:

1. How much money one has or makes
2. How much someone paid for something
3. Sexual subjects
4. Class status or racial issues
5. A person's age
6. A person's weight

These are very sensitive subjects because Americans take them very personally. Even though you do not mean to offend them, they may be upset if you ask these questions.

Sample of an Offensive Conversation

MARY ANN: Hello, my name is Mary Ann.

PAULA: Hi, I'm Paula

MARY ANN: I really like your dress. How much did it cost?

PAULA: Well, uh, I don't remember for sure.

MARY ANN: Your shoes are nice, too. How much were they? Did you get them on sale?

PAULA: I have to be going now. See you later.

Why didn't Paula tell Mary Ann how much her dress and shoes cost? What do you think Paula's body language was when Mary Ann asked her questions? Why did Paula leave so quickly after meeting her? What could Mary Ann have talked about instead? Paula was annoyed by Mary Ann's questions. She probably remembered how much the clothes cost but didn't want to tell Mary Ann. She told her a *white lie*, an untruth that doesn't hurt anyone.

LET'S SHARE

To compare acceptable and unacceptable topics of conversation in the United States with those from your country, fill in this chart. When you have finished, share this information with your fellow class members.

In _____
(name of your country)

Acceptable Topics of Conversation	*Unacceptable Topics of Conversation*
1. _____	1. _____
2. _____	2. _____
3. _____	3. _____
4. _____	4. _____
5. _____	5. _____

Look at these topics carefully? What are the differences between American topics and topics from your country? What does this tell you about the people of both countries?

Here are some more pointers about conversation. When you are talking with your friend, listen carefully and let the conversation continue. Don't just ask one question after another or answer your friend's questions with one-word answers. In America, as in most countries, people feel uneasy if you ask a lot of questions or answer in one-word replies. They will think that you are being "pushy" or that you are uninterested in what they have to say. Be prepared to tell about yourself and your interests as well as to ask about the other person. In this way, both you and your listener can share information and learn about each other. You should also be aware that Americans are uncomfortable with silence in conversation and will always try to think of something to say to fill the gap. However, you may feel very comfortable with silence.

NOW YOU DO IT

Choose an identity you would like as your own—that of a famous movie star, a world leader, an ambassador, a teacher, or a musician, for example. Write your new name and occupation on a sheet of paper. Below this, write your real name. Give this paper to the teacher.

In the minisimulation below you will pretend that you and your classmates are at a party at a friend's house. Using your new name, introduce yourself to two other people and learn their names and occupations. Then introduce them to each other. When you introduce them, be sure to tell each what the other person does so that they can make small talk.

Example:

HEATHER: Hello, I'm Heather Allen.

SUSAN: Hello, I'm Susan Miselli. It's nice to meet you.

HEATHER: Same here. Do you know Steven Johnson? He and I sell computers.

SUSAN: No. (*shakes hands*) How do you do. That sounds like interesting work.

STEVEN: Yes, it is. I've been working for Computer Installations for four years in the Hardware Division.

SUSAN: Do you sell personal or business computers?

STEVEN: Mostly personal computers. You wouldn't believe how much the industry has changed in the last year!

SUSAN: What's happened? . . .

(A third person, Molly, joins Heather and Susan. Steven has gone to talk with another friend.)

MOLLY: Hello, Heather.

HEATHER: Hi, Molly.

MOLLY: How are you?

HEATHER: Fine. Do you know Susan?

MOLLY: No, I don't.

HEATHER: Molly, this is Susan Miselli. Susan, this is Molly Blair.

SUSAN: Pleased to meet you.

MOLLY: Same here.

HEATHER: Susan is a singer.

MOLLY: Where do you sing?

SUSAN: Well, I'm studying music right now, but I hope some day to sing at the Metropolitan Opera House.

MOLLY: That's wonderful. I hope you get that opportunity.

SUSAN: Thank you. What do you do?

MOLLY: I'm an electrical engineer. I work at the same company as Heather.

What might Susan say to continue the conversation?

Mini-simulation

Now that you know about small talk and have read the example, you are ready for the mini-simulation. You have 15 minutes to accomplish this. Follow the same directions under the **NOW YOU DO IT** section. Use the name and profession you wrote down and gave to your teacher to make your introductions. Most of the time at social functions where there are many people, the guests stand and talk briefly to a lot of people. If possible, either move the furniture in your room to the side or gather in the front of the room.

Discussion Questions

At the end of the simulation, discuss the following questions.

1. Were you able to meet two or more people? How many did you meet?
2. Introduce to the class one of the people you met. Give his or her name and occupation.
3. Did making introductions become easier for you? Why?
4. What kind of small talk did you make? Did you talk about professions, weather, the news?
5. Did you have any problems? What were they?

SUMMARY

By comparing the customs and cultures of people from other countries, we can learn how others view the world and why they think the way they do. By understanding others, we not only can form deeper friendships with others but can also learn more about ourselves and our own culture. Think carefully about your answers to these questions.

1. In what significant ways do the gestures and body language of your country differ from those of the United States?
2. In what ways do the gestures and body language of your country resemble those of the United States?
3. How are the customs for making conversation in the United States different from those in your country?
4. Which customs for making conversation in the United States are the same as in your country?
5. What other country did you learn about? What was especially interesting to you about that country?
6. Which of the American customs that you have studied do you find difficult to deal with? Why?
7. Which American customs seem the most natural to you? Why?

two
Attending School

Cultures have developed a particular style of teaching. Therefore, moving from one country to another to study may present some surprises.

In some cultures, it is rude for students to ask their teachers questions. Questioning the teacher is like saying the teacher has not done a good job explaining the subject. In some cultures, students learn through rote memorization, and what the teacher says is always the truth. In other cultures, students are taught to think for themselves. The role of the teacher is to stimulate their thinking, to get them to ask questions, challenge, and even argue with the teacher, and to come to their own conclusions.

In some parts of the world, grades depend on the status of one's family and not on one's ability with the subject.

Some studies indicate that people like to learn differently. Some people learn better by listening, while others need to see the information. Your answers to the questions below may give you some idea of how you prefer to learn. When you have finished, compare your answers with those of other people in your class.

1. I prefer to learn by listening to the teacher lecture. (Yes or no)
2. I prefer to learn by reading and studying my texts. (Yes or no)
3. I prefer to learn by studying or working with other people. (Yes or no)
4. I prefer to study by myself. (Yes or no)
5. I like to ask the teacher questions. (Yes or no)
6. When I study for a test, I
   a. read my notes
   b. say my notes aloud
   c. rewrite my notes
7. I remember best
   a. smells
   b. tastes
   c. sounds
   d. sights
   e. touches

8. If I received as a gift a machine with many buttons on it, I would
   a. read the directions first
   b. play with the buttons first
   c. ask someone to show me how it works
9. I like to
   a. memorize facts
   b. think about ideas
10. This is how people are taught in my culture. (Explain)

In this chapter, we will share information about attending school in our own countries and learn some of the customs for being successful in American schools.

1 LEARNING ABOUT AMERICAN SCHOOLS

Before we discuss schools in the United States, let's take a few minutes to discuss schools in your country. Meet in a group with three or four other students and share information about schools you have attended in your country. Use these questions as a guide for your discussion.

1. What do students wear to school?
2. How do students get to school?
3. How do students know which class to go to? Are there different classes, or does everyone study in one room?
4. How do students greet the teacher? What do they say? What body language do they use? Do they stand?
5. How does the teacher greet the students?
6. Do students bring gifts to the teacher? If so, when?
7. How do students address the teacher: Mr., Ms., Mrs., Dr., Professor, Teacher, or by his or her first name?
8. When does the school year begin? How long does it last? How long is the school day?
9. Who decides what a student will study?
10. Who decides which students will attend college and what they will study? Why?

As you work through this chapter, compare the customs in your country with those in the United States.

QUICK CUSTOMS QUIZ

Below are situations in which you might find yourself in the United States. Read each situation, decide what is appropriate, and choose the answer that best fits the circumstances. Draw a circle around the letter in front of your answer. Check your answers against those on page 161, which are the answers an American would probably give.

1. Your teacher, Mrs. Bills, is walking past you in the hallway and you wish to catch her attention and say hello. What is the best way to do this?

    a. Say, "Hello, Teacher."
    b. Wave your hand.
    c. Smile and say, "Hello, Mrs. Bills."

2. You have not done well on a paper, and your professor has called you into his office to speak to you about your poor grade. When he speaks to you, what should you do?

    a. Look directly into his eyes.
    b. Look down at the floor.
    c. Look up at the ceiling.
    d. Focus your eyes on a distant object.

3. Your math professor has been explaining a problem in class. You understand the first half of the explanation, but you do not understand the rest of the problem. What should you do?

    a. Raise your hand and tell the professor that you don't understand. Ask him or her to explain the problem again.
    b. Wait until after class and speak to the professor.
    c. After class, ask a friend to explain the problem to you.
    d. Do not ask anyone because this is very embarrassing.
    e. Forget about the problem. You probably will not need to know it anyway.

4. You have an appointment to see your adviser at 10:30 Tuesday morning. On Monday, you develop a fever of 102 degrees Fahrenheit and are clearly too sick to keep your appointment. What should you do?

    a. Call the adviser immediately and cancel the appointment.
    b. Nothing.
    c. Go even though you are very sick. It would be rude not to go.
    d. Ask a friend or roommate to keep the appointment for you.
    e. Write your adviser a note.

5. You are in college and find that you are not doing well in a course. You feel that you are not doing well because you have taken too many courses and are not able to complete all the required assignments. What should you do?

    a. Stop going to class because you don't have time to do the work.
    b. Continue the courses and get your friends to finish your assignments.
    c. See your adviser and ask if you can drop the course.
    d. Speak to the instructor and ask for a grade of "incomplete" so that you can finish the course work during the next semester.

6. You have been doing well in all your classes except social studies. You have the feeling that the teacher doesn't like you. What should you do?

    a. Stop going to class.
    b. Go to class only to take tests.
    c. Speak to your guidance counselor.
    d. Do the best you can under the circumstances.
    e. Speak to the teacher.

7. Your teacher has explained that he determines your grade as follows:

Quizzes	10%
Tests	40%
Reports	30%
Class participation	20%

You do not like to answer or ask questions in class. What should you do?

    a. Ask to speak to the teacher and explain your shyness.
    b. Tell the teacher you do not think it is fair to put so much emphasis on class participation.
    c. Do nothing.

8. While you are taking an examination, you see someone leaning over to copy your paper. What should you do?

    a. Move your paper closer so that he or she can see.
    b. Tell your professor.
    c. Cover your paper so the other person can't see it.
    d. Tell the other person in a loud voice to stop cheating.

9. You have just received a test paper back from your teacher. She has marked as wrong an answer that you believe to be right because there is another way to interpret the question. What should you do?

    a. Nothing. The teacher should never be questioned.
    b. Raise your hand and ask why your interpretation is wrong.
    c. Speak to the teacher after class.
    d. Complain to the principal or to your parents.

10. You are in history class and the teacher asks for a definition of *free enterprise*. You know the answer. What should you do?

    a. Raise your hand and wait to be called on.
    b. Do not answer the question. That would be showing off.
    c. Wait for the eldest and most respected member of the class to answer.

11. Your teacher has just announced a big test for next Friday. That day is a very holy day in your religion, and you intended to stay home to celebrate it. What should you do?

a. Raise your hand and, when recognized, tell the teacher that Friday is a religious holiday and you won't be in school. Ask the teacher to change the test date.
b. Come to school and take the test.
c. Be absent and miss the test.
d. Go up to the teacher after class and explain the situation.

Discussion Questions

1. Choose one question and tell how the answer would be different in your culture.
2. Which of these questions is the most difficult for you to do or to understand? Why?
3. Are teachers perceived differently in your culture? How? What is the role of the teacher in your country?

2 RULES FOR ATTENDING SCHOOL

These are the rules for attending school in the United States. Indicate whether they are also true in your country by putting a check (✔) in the appropriate column.

Rule	Also True in Your Country?
Kindergarten through high school 1. Always refer to a teacher title and last name: Dr. Walker, Mr. Fields, Mrs. Ramirez, Professor McGuinness (never call a teacher "Teacher.")	
2. Arrive to class on time or a little early.	
3. Raise your hand when you want to ask a question.	
4. You may speak to the teacher from your desk while you are seated.	
5. When you are absent, you must make up the work you have missed. Ask either the teacher or a classmate for the work.	
6. If you expect to be away from school because of an emergency, tell your teacher in advance and ask for the work you will miss.	
7. All assignments you hand in must be your own work.	
8. Never cheat on a test.	

Box continued on following page

Rule	Also True in Your Country?
9. If you are having difficulty with a class, schedule an appointment to see the teacher for help. The teacher will be glad to help you.	
10. Students must bring a note from a parent explaining any absence or tardiness.	
11. The only acceptable excuse for absence is personal illness, a death in the family, or a religious holiday. It is illegal to stay home from school for any other reason.	
12. When a teacher asks a question and does not name a particular student to answer it, anyone who knows the answer should raise one hand.	
College 1. A student who receives a failing grade in a course usually needs to repeat the course.	
2. Students are expected to work hard in their courses.	
3. Students' work is not discussed with parents without the students' permission.	
4. After taking the required courses in their major, students may select their other courses.	
5. All students are considered equal in the classroom and are judged only by the quality of their work.	
6. Students alone are responsible for their progress in a course. They must seek help, either with the professor or in a lab, if they need help with the work.	
7. Any student who has the ability and the desire may apply to college.	

After you have completed this assignment, be prepared to discuss your responses with your classmates. Consider how you would feel in an American class and why. Choose items on the list that you would have the most difficulty accepting. Explain why these would be hard for you. Also be prepared to explain which items you would do differently in your country and what the rules are for correct conduct in your country.

LET'S SHARE

By comparing the customs and cultures of people from other countries and the way they educate their children, we can gain insights into how they view the world and why they think the way they do. By understanding others, we can also learn more about ourselves. Answer these questions after you have carefully thought about your answers.

1. What are the most important ways in which school in your country differs from school in the United States?

2. In what significant ways are school in your country and school in the United States alike?
3. How are students' attitudes toward teachers and school in the two countries different?
4. What would happen in your country if students acted the way American students do?
5. Grades are often calculated differently, not only in different countries, but also in the same country. Generally, in the United States, teachers consider the following areas when computing grades:

Tests: formal examinations
Quizzes: short tests, sometimes given to students without telling them in advance
Homework: work that the students are expected to do individually at home
Class participation: active involvement in the class by asking and answering questions
Research paper: a written report that requires looking up information in the library
Attendance: going to class every time it meets
Promptness: coming to class at exactly the time the class is scheduled to begin and handing in work when it is due
Attitude: showing interest in the class and respect for the teacher, the subject, and the other students

Are these areas also important in your country? Which ones are not important?
6. Schools in the United States use their own grading system. However, most grades are either letter grades (A, B, C, D, F) or number grades. (Please note that in some schools the letter/number grade may vary by one or two points.)

Letter Grade	Number Equivalent	Meaning	
A	90–100	Excellent	
B	80–89	Good	
C	70–79	Average	Passing
D	60–69	Poor	
F	0–59	Failing	

What grading system is used in your country? How does it compare with grading in the United States?

Grade in Your Country	Meaning	U.S. Equivalent

29

7. Here are the grades an American student received. What kind of a student is he? In which areas does he need to improve?

English	C
Math	B
Science	D
Social studies	B
Physical education	A
Spanish	F

8. Form pairs. One person tells the other what is different about the grading system of his or her country. The person listening must then repeat this information to his or her partner. Then switch roles. This is a good way to improve your listening skills and learn about another culture.

IDIOMS

Here are some idioms commonly used by students in school. Match the idiom with its meaning. Check your answers on page 161.

_____ 1. Cut the chatter; button your lip

A. Sit down

_____ 2. Move it! hop to it!

B. In a difficult situation

_____ 3. Grab a seat

C. All of you in the group

_____ 4. To run something into the ground

D. To overdo something

_____ 5. In hot water; up the creek

E. Move quickly

_____ 6. To put in an all-nighter; to burn the midnight oil

F. To admire someone

_____ 7. Darn! drat! phooey! rats!

G. To think one is better than someone else

_____ 8. Toughie; bad news

H. Difficult

_____ 9. You guys

I. To study all night for a test

_____ 10. To look down on someone

J. Expressions that show disappointment

_____ 11. To look up to someone

K. To locate information in a book or magazine

_____ 12. To look something up   L. Stop talking

_____ 13. To help out   M. To assist with a project; to provide information

3 HOLDING YOUR OWN IN CONVERSATIONS

Now that we've discussed American schools and how they compare to schools in your culture, let's talk about "holding your own" in conversations with friends. Let's examine some typical conversations you might hear among students in a high school or college. Pay careful attention to the blank spaces so that you can fill in the dialogue correctly.

Complete these dialogues. Then role-play them, using correct and expressive body language and gestures.

1. You and your friend are on one of the teams at school (football, soccer, lacrosse, etc.).

FRIEND: I'm not in the mood to play today.

YOU: _____

FRIEND: Well, I was out late last night and _____.

YOU: _____

FRIEND: OK. Let's go.
(You and your friend arrive at practice. You are in the locker room.)

FRIEND: I wonder how many laps we'll have to do.

YOU: _____

FRIEND: The coach really likes to run us into the ground!

YOU: _____

FRIEND: Last semester, some kid gave him trouble and he had to run around the track thirty times!

YOU: _____

2. You and your friend leave the locker room and head for the playing field.

Coach: OK, hurry up! Move it! Let's go, you guys!

You: (whispering to your friend) _____

Friend: He's really in a rotten mood today, all right!

Coach: _____

You: Forty laps! That'll take all afternoon!

31

Friend: _____

Coach: Cut the chatter and hop to it!

3. You're sitting in the library when a friend approaches you.

FRIEND: Hi. Have you seen Juan Carlos?

YOU: _____

FRIEND: Oh no! He owes me three dollars and I need the money to pick up some tickets for next week's rock concert.

YOU: _____

FRIEND: You will? Thanks!

4. You walk into the cafeteria at school feeling very upset because you got a low score on a test. You see your friends and walk over to their table.

FRIEND 1: Hi, there. Why don't you grab a seat? I have to go to class.

YOU: _____

FRIEND 2: Hey, you look kind of down.

YOU: _____

FRIEND 2: Don't worry about it. Mr. Calderwood always drops the lowest test grade.

YOU: _____

FRIEND 3: Yeah. I had him last year and he did the same thing then.

YOU: _____

5. You and a friend are talking in the school corridor about a test you've just taken.

YOU: _____

SUSAN: Yes, it really was a tough test.

YOU: _____

SUSAN: I think I passed, but I'm not sure.

YOU: _____

SUSAN: Yeah! Well, we'll find out for sure on Thursday.

YOU: _____

SUSAN: See you later. I told Jennifer I'd meet her at the bus stop at three o'clock.

YOU: _____

SUSAN: Take it easy. 'Bye.

ROLE PLAY

With a partner, prepare a dialogue for each of the following situations. Be prepared to role-play each of the situations before the class.

1. You are away at college and have just received a telephone call that a close relative is very ill. You are upset and can't study. Finally you decide that you must go home. Role-play your conversation with your teacher in which you explain that you must return home.
2. You don't understand the word *invertebrate*, which your biology teacher has been using. Role-play raising your hand and asking what it means. Do the same for the term *laissez faire* in social studies and the difference between *induction* and *deduction* in math. The person playing the part of the teacher must look up the word in the dictionary and be able to answer questions about it.
3. You are visiting your child's teacher on parent-teacher conference day. Be prepared to ask how your child is doing: Is your child having any problem with class work? Does your child get along with the other children? Is your child well behaved in class? And so on.

4 IDIOMS AND PHRASES

In the United States, students are expected to participate actively in their classes. They are expected to ask and answer questions. Students can also ask brief questions in class or see the teacher privately for extra help or lengthier explanations of class material. To ask questions and get information, you need to know idioms and phrases used to seek information. Please study the following brief dialogues before proceeding. Notice that some are appropriate to the classroom, where you ask questions which would be of interest to the class. Others are used in the privacy of the teacher's office, when you want to discuss something that is related to you personally.

In class:

1. You: I'm not sure I understand. Will you please repeat that?
   Teacher: Yes, I said that . . .

2. You: Please say that again more slowly. I didn't get what you said.
   Teacher: I said . . .

3. You: Would you mind rewording that?
   Teacher: No. I said . . .

4. You: Excuse me. Do you mean that . . . ?
   Teacher: Yes, that's correct.

In the teacher's office:

1. You: Do you have a minute?
   Teacher: I can't talk right now. How about tomorrow at this time?
   You: Fine. See you then.

2. You: Can you tell me how I'm doing in class?
   Teacher: I'd be happy to.

3. You: I'm having trouble with the essay. Do you have any suggestions about organization?
   Teacher: Yes, limit your topic and decide on your main ideas.
   You: That's really helpful. I certainly understand it better now. Thank you.
   Teacher: You're welcome. Come again whenever you need help. See you in class.

4. You: How can I improve my work?
   Teacher: You could . . .
   You: What other changes do you suggest?
   Teacher: I think you should . . .

To a professor's secretary:

You: Excuse me.

Secretary: Yes, what do you want?

You: I need to speak to Professor Miller.

Secretary: Just a moment. I'll tell the professor you're here.

NOW YOU DO IT

Often students need to ask the teacher questions to find out more about the subject or to help them understand the lesson. Read the following dialogues, and for each, compose a question that a student could ask the teacher.

1. The class has been discussing school.

Teacher: And that's how students act in the United States.

You: _____

Teacher: That's an excellent question. Can anyone answer it?

Classmate: _____

Teacher: Good answer! Can anyone add to her answer?

Notice that in the United States, teachers often ask other students in the class to supply the answers to questions instead of always giving the answer themselves.

2. Your class has been discussing major rivers in the United States. You want to know how long the Mississippi River is.

YOU: _____

PROFESSOR: I'm not sure exactly how long the Mississippi River is. Why don't you look it up in the encyclopedia and tell the class tomorrow?

Teachers in the United States are not uncomfortable saying they don't know the answer to a question. However, sometimes instead of answering the questions, they will encourage students to think for themselves by asking them to find the answer.

3. Students in the United States are interested in getting high grades. A passing mark of C is often not acceptable to them. Students who feel that a grade is unfairly low may ask the instructor why they received a particular grade on a paper and how they can improve their work.

TEACHER: Hello, Jim. Can I help you?

JIM: _____

TEACHER: The reason you received a low grade was that your paper was not well organized and contained many spelling and grammar mistakes.

JIM: _____

TEACHER: If you want to improve your organization, make an outline before you write your paper. Read each sentence carefully to find mistakes in grammar and spelling. You may wish to have a friend help you find errors.

JIM: _____

TEACHER: I'm glad that will help you. Come to me before you hand in your next paper and we'll go over it together.

HOLDING YOUR OWN IN CLASS

Conduct in the classroom in the United States may be quite different from behavior you are accustomed to. In the United States, class participation is often considered important. Teachers respect a student's right to ask questions, and some teachers even play "devil's advocate" to encourage students to think for themselves. To do this, instructors use a variety of methods to get information from their students.

In these dialogues, you will find typical questioning techniques American teachers use. Fill in the dialogue using the sentences below it. When you finish, check your answers on page 162.

Model Dialogues/Matching

1. A teacher is discussing free speech in a sociology class.

TEACHER: Define *free speech*.

YOU: _____

TEACHER: What do you mean by that?

YOU: _____

TEACHER: Can you explain it further?

YOU: _____

TEACHER: Give me an example, please.

YOU: _____

    A. In the United States, you can say you disagree with the President.
    B. Even the newspaper can criticize the President.
    C. Free speech means that people can say whatever they want.
    D. You can criticize the government and nothing will happen to you.

2. A political science class is studying the United Nations.

TEACHER: How has the United Nations changed in the past ten years?

STUDENT 1: _____

TEACHER: Can anyone help?

STUDENT 2: _____

TEACHER: Very good. Has the UN changed in any other way?

STUDENT 3: _____

    A. More Third World countries belong to the United Nations now.
    B. I'm not sure.
    C. Yes, the Third World countries can outvote some of the larger nations.

5 SIMULATION GAME: ATTENDING SCHOOL*

During this game, your teacher will tell you which of the following approaches to use.

1. Play the "in the classroom" part first and then play the "in the hall" part.

*For detailed rules, see the Appendix.

2. Divide into two groups and have one group play the "in the classroom" part while the other group plays the "in the hall" part. After ten minutes, the groups change and complete the other part of the game.

3. Divide into two groups. While one group is doing the activities, the other group observes the players and evaluates their responses using the evaluation form on pages 39 and 40. Then the two groups switch roles.

4. Act as a teacher by preparing a short lesson for the class on one of the topics your teacher assigns. Several students may take turns being the teacher during the game. As teacher, you may call on students or answer their questions. You will receive 10 points for being teacher, but while you are teacher, you cannot receive points for any other activities.

Scoring

Usually students sign for each other to get points after completing activities, but during the classroom discussion, players may sign for themselves when they complete activities 1, 2, and 4. No activity may be repeated more than once for points.

Game Setup

For the "in the classroom" activities, you will need a regular classroom arrangement with enough chairs for all participants who will be playing this part of the game.

For the "in the hall" activities, choose one part of your classroom to be the hall. Remove all the chairs and pretend that you are in the hall between classes.

POINT ACTIVITIES

In the Classroom

Note: During this section, the teacher may hold a class discussion over material the class is familiar with or begin another short lesson over new material. If your teacher wishes, he or she may ask a student to "teach" a five-minute lesson to the class. This student may talk about customs in his or her country, comment on American culture, or discuss a topic of the teacher's choice.

If your teacher chooses to do optional activity 6, you will be asked to form groups of three or four to discuss a topic. When you have finished, decide as a group who should get points for each activity.

1. You do not understand the explanation the teacher has given. Ask the teacher to explain the problem in another way.

   Point value: 3   Signature _____

2. Your teacher asks you a questions. Answer it.

   Point value: 2   Signature _____

3. Give a two-minute speech to your class on a subject your teacher assigns. Raise your hand to volunteer.

   Point value: 5   Signature _____

4. Ask a student a question about the presentation given in activity 3.

   Point value: 2   Signature _____

   Answer the question that the student has asked you about your presentation.

   Point value: 2   Signature _____

5. You see another student trying to copy your paper. Decide on the best way to deal with the situation and carry it out.

   Point value: 2   Signature _____

6. (Optional Activity) Your teacher asks your class to form groups of three or four to discuss one of these topics:
   a. Women's liberation in the United States
   b. The difference between American schools and schools in your country
   c. The effects of divorce on the family
   d. The true meaning of *freedom*
   e. A topic your teacher assigns

   As a group, agree upon and write out four statements about your topic that you can share with your class. You have ten minutes to complete this activity.

   Point value: 2   Signature _____

   The following points will be awarded for participation with the discussion group. Group members will decide how many points each student gets.

   a. Serving as group leader: 3 points
   b. Contributing information about the topic: 2 points
   c. Listening to others talk without interrupting or criticizing their information: 3 points
   d. Showing through body language that you are interested in what the other people have to say: 4 points
   e. Asking questions to encourage participation or to get another student to clarify what he or she has said: 2 points

In the Hall

7. You see a fellow student in the hall. Ask him or her for the homework assignment.

   Point value: 2   Signature _____

8. Ask someone out for Saturday night. Agree on where you'll go, when you'll leave and return, and how you should dress.

   Point value: 4   Signature _____

9. Someone asks you on a date. Accept graciously.

   Point value: 2   Signature _____

10. You ask someone or someone asks you to go on a date or to a party. One of you pretends to have another date on that night but would like to go out at another time. Be very considerate of the other person's feelings and try to arrange for a date at another time.

    Point value: 4   Signature _____

11. Carry on a conversation with a friend for at least three minutes about something that happened at school.

    Point value: 2   Signature _____

12. Ask a friend to explain a class assignment to you.

    Point value: 2   Signature _____

13. You are getting ready to register for the next semester. Ask one of your classmates about one of the courses that he or she has taken.

    Point value: 2   Signature _____

OBSERVER'S CHECKLIST

Evaluate players' gestures, language usage, and idioms as they work through the activities. Write the player's name in the first box and note the number of the activity he or she is participating in. Then rate how the player performed the activity, writing a + if the person used English, idioms, and gestures correctly or a − if the person needs to improve. Make helpful comments or observations for the player in the comments column.

Player's Name	Activity Number	English Usage	Idioms	Gestures	Comments

Box continued on following page

Player's Name	Activity Number	English Usage	Idioms	Gestures	Comments

three

Building Friendships

Some people, when they first arrive in the United States, say that Americans are very friendly, but after living in the United States for a while, they change their minds. One international student explained that when he first came, people were very friendly. They helped him get settled, took him shopping, invited him for dinner, and called to see how he was. After two or three weeks, however, they stopped doing these things, and he was confused and disappointed.

Americans tend to do what is necessary to help people when they first arrive. They "go all out" doing many things to help the others get settled and often make the new arrivals feel like a part of the family. The newcomers expect this warm hospitality to continue in the form of a solid friendship. However, Americans expect that once people are settled and have been here for a few weeks, they will begin to do things for themselves and become independent.

Like other aspects of culture, friendship is perceived differently in various parts of the world. In this chapter, we will discuss friends, neighbors, and acquaintances. We will talk about how to make friends in the United States and how to communicate with them during both troublesome and happy times. As we discuss friendship in the United States, compare it with friendship as it is practiced in your culture. Share this information with your classmates.

1 FRIENDSHIPS ACROSS CULTURES

IDIOMS AND EXPRESSIONS

Here is a list of common idioms and expressions used in the United States to describe friends and friendship. Can you explain what each means? Do you have similar expressions in your language? Check your answers on page 162.

Idiom	Definition
1. Fair-weather friend	
2. Lady friend	
3. Girlfriend/boyfriend	
4. Blood brothers	
5. Birds of a feather flock together.	
6. One rotten apple spoils the whole bunch.	
7. A friend in need is a friend indeed.	
8. Familiarity breeds contempt.	

Now list idioms and expressions associated with friendship in your language. Translate them into English and then share them with the class.

	Your Language	English Translation
1.		
2.		
3.		
4.		

ANALYSIS

The word *friend* in the United States has a broad meaning, including everyone from a casual acquaintance to a long-time best friend. The following chart describes some of these levels of friendship.

Term	Definition	Customary Behavior
Neighbor	Someone who lives next door, across the street, or on the same block	Neighbors generally say hello when they see each other. Some become good friends. They often help each other, borrow things, and watch each other's houses when no one is home.
Acquaintance	Someone you have been introduced to but do not know well	Acquaintances generally say hello when they meet and make small talk.
Best friend	Someone you can rely on and would feel comfortable asking for assistance at any time	Best friends generally share good and bad times together and spend free time together.
Boyfriend/girlfriend	Someone of the opposite sex for whom you have romantic feelings	Go on dates, share affection, walk arm in arm in public.

Box continued on following page

Box continued from preceding page

Term	Definition	Customary Behavior
Girlfriend	A female friend of another woman (men and boys do not refer to their male friends as boyfriends)	Spend time together and share common interests.
Classmate	A student in your class	Classmates say hello, make small talk, and sometimes study together.
Business associate or colleague	Someone who works in the same place of business as you do	Colleagues share business information, discuss problems related to their work, and occasionally socialize.

LET'S SHARE

1. Describe the type of relationship people in your country have with:

   Neighbors   _____

   _____

   _____

   Acquaintances   _____

   _____

   _____

   Best friends   _____

   _____

   _____

   Boyfriends/
   girlfriends   _____

   _____

   _____

2. Are there other categories of friendship in your culture? Please explain. Share this information with fellow class members.

   _____

   _____

   _____

3. Now that we have discussed friends and the different levels of friendship, take a few minutes to think about your friends at home in your country.

    Working in pairs, find out from your partner the answers to the following questions:
    a. Who is your partner's best friend?
    b. What makes this friend so special?
    c. Was there one thing this friend did that showed him or her to be a true friend?
    d. What does your partner remember best about this friend?
    e. Ask your partner to tell you about an especially important experience that he or she shared with this special friend.

    When you have finished, report to the class the answers to questions 2 and 3. Are there any similarities or differences in people's answers to these questions? Do different cultures view and deal with friendship in unique ways?

2 IMAGE

In Chapter One, we talked about body language and gestures. Now let's consider your image, that is, the way that you appear to others. Clothes, hairstyles, makeup, cleanliness, posture, and even a person's name tell you a great deal about a person.

    Look at the pictures and decide how you feel about each person. Use these questions as a guide:

A

B

C

D

E

F

G

1. Would you like to have this person as a friend or relative? Why or why not?
2. What do you think the person in the photograph is like? Consider descriptions like fun-loving, proper, educated, respected, well behaved, poor, honest, friendly, weak, sad. What gives you this impression?

Your conclusions about these people may or may not be true. We call such conclusions *stereotypes*. You apply a stereotype when you decide what a person is like before you actually know him or her personally.

LET'S SHARE

1. What personal characteristics do people in your culture admire and respect (i.e., dress, appearance, friendliness)?
2. What is your idea of a "beautiful" person? Discuss this person physically, intellectually, and emotionally. Form groups of three and discuss

the ways that your ideals are the same or different. Why do people have different ideas of beauty?

3. How do stereotypes limit our opportunities to meet and learn from other people and situations?

HYGIENE

As you have just seen, appearance plays an important part, rightly or wrongly, in the way we feel about people. Therefore, it is very important to make a good first impression. However, the feeling that people get when meeting one another for the first time is not just based on how one looks.

Look at the items on this list. What do they have in common?

Spray deodorant
Roll-on deodorant
Odor Eaters
Breath mints
Chewing gum
Mouthwash

All of these products are used to prevent body odors. Americans are offended if a person smells of sweat or has bad breath. Showering daily, as most Americans do, is not sufficient to prevent body odor (or "B.O.," as it is called). Because Americans are so sensitive to odor, they use a deodorant under their arms, brush their teeth twice a day, and use breath fresheners when they believe their breath smells stale, after smoking, or after eating onions or garlic. Clothes, especially shirts and blouses, are washed after one or two wearings, even if they appear to be clean.

LET'S SHARE

Sight, sound, taste, touch, and hearing play an important role in how we perceive another culture. (Remember the optical illusions in Chapter One and our discussion of perception?) List the sights, sounds, tastes, and smells that remind you most strongly of your family or hometown.

1. Sights: _____

_____

2. Sounds: _____

_____

3. Tastes: _____

_____

4. Smells: _____

_____

3 SHARING GOOD TIMES

Friends are people with whom we share both good and bad times. We share happiness, excitement, anxiety, and sadness with them. This chapter is made up of exercises and conversations that contain idioms and expressions used to convey and share these emotions. In this section, you will be asked to work with a partner in developing a dialogue based on a particular situation to express one of these feelings.

EXCITEMENT

Sharing your joys and happiness is one of the most pleasant parts of friendship. The conversations that follow contain many expressions commonly used to express excitement.

Model Dialogues

1. PERSON A: I can't believe it! I got an A on my science test!
   PERSON B: Congratulations! That's great!
   A: Thanks. I'm so happy! I really worked hard for that A.
   B: I know you did. You deserve it.

2. A: I have the most wonderful news!
   B: What happened?
   A: My sister finally had a baby girl. After all, she has three boys!
   B: How wonderful!

3. A: You'll never believe this!
   B: What happened?
   A: I won five dollars in the school raffle! How about that!
   B: Boy, are you lucky!

NOW YOU DO IT

Complete these conversations, using what you have learned in this chapter. After your instructor has checked your work, role-play them with a partner.

1. MARK: I can't believe it!
   YOU: What _____
   MARK: The coach is putting me in the starting lineup for this Saturday's football game!
   YOU: _____

2. YOU: Guess what?
   SUE: _____
   YOU: Robert asked me out for Saturday night.
   SUE: _____
   YOU: _____

3. JENNIFER: _____
   YOU: _____
   JENNIFER: I got a job!
   YOU: _____
   JENNIFER: I start work Monday.
   YOU: _____

4. YOU: _____
   PAUL: Dr. O'Neill postponed the test in physics until Monday!
   YOU: _____
   PAUL: You're not kidding! Now I can go skiing this weekend.

Form groups of four or five. As a group, come up with two situations that would cause excitement and two that would cause worry. Then write a dialogue to go with each situation. After your teacher has checked your work, role-play them for the class. Be sure to use gestures, body language, and facial expressions as well as words to convey your meaning.

SHARING DIFFICULT TIMES

WORRY

Worry is a common feeling and one that can be alleviated by sharing with friends. People respond to worry in many ways. Some people become irritable, others become very quiet and intense, and still others may become sad and distracted. Look at the photograph on page 50. It shows a person who is worried. Notice her gestures, body language, and facial expression. What makes this person look worried?

Model Dialogues

Here are some ways to express and to respond to worry.

1. PERSON A: I'm so upset.
   PERSON B: What's the matter? What happened?

2. A: I really need to talk to you. Do you have a minute?
   B: Sure. What's bothering you?

3. A: I have a real problem. I don't know what to do!
   B: What seems to be the trouble? How can I help you?

ROLE PLAY

Read these sample dialogues. Then, using correct gestures, facial expressions, and body language, role-play them with a partner.

JANE: What's wrong? You really look worried and upset.
SARAH: My dog was hit by a car.
JANE: I'm sorry to hear that. Is he OK?
SARAH: I don't know. He's at the vet's.
JANE: I hope he'll be all right.
SARAH: Thank you. So do I.

TOM: I'm so worried. I haven't heard from my family in three months.
ADAM: How often do they usually write?
TOM: Oh, at least once a month. Either my mother or my father writes.
ADAM: The mail is really slow sometimes. I'm sure you'll hear from them soon.
TOM: I hope so.

ADAM: You know the saying, "No news is good news." If something were wrong, they'd have contacted you.

TOM: Maybe you're right. Thanks, Adam.

NOW YOU DO IT

Choose two of the six dialogues and complete them with a partner. When your teacher has checked your work, act them out for the class.

1. Jim, who is 17 years old looks upset. See if you can find out what is bothering him.

YOU: _____

JIM: Oh. I had an argument with my father.

YOU: _____

JIM: I told him I was going to Alan's party Saturday night and that I would be home at three in the morning.

YOU: _____

JIM: He got angry because I didn't ask him. I told him.

YOU: _____

JIM: He said I couldn't go at all. He said that three in the morning was much too late.

YOU: _____

JIM: I said everyone was staying out that late.

YOU: _____

JIM: Maybe you're right. Maybe he'll change his mind.

2. Your neighbor, Mary, is 27 years old. Her daughter Ellen is 6 years old and is in the first grade. It is 4 o'clock and Ellen hasn't come home from school yet. She is usually home at 3 o'clock. You see Mary walking up and down the street outside of her house. Find out what is wrong and comfort her.

YOU: (*ask what's wrong*) _____

MARY: _____

YOU: (*show concern*) _____

MARY: _____

YOU: Maybe Ellen went to a friend's house.

MARY: _____

51

3. Mike, a friend of yours, has been working at a factory for three years. Today you meet him on the street and notice he seems unhappy. Ask what is wrong and show concern when he tells you the problem.

MIKE: Hi!

YOU: _____

MIKE: Not so good. I need to talk.

YOU: _____

MIKE: I just came from work. They announced today that they would be laying people off.

YOU: _____

MIKE: Everyone is very worried.

YOU: _____

MIKE: _____

YOU: _____

4. Your friend Bob is 16 years old. You see him sitting in the principal's office at school. After school, you talk to him.

YOU: _____

BOB: I'm in big trouble.

YOU: _____

BOB: I came into class late and Mrs. Abbott started yelling at me. She told me I had to get a pass and she would see me at detention. I said, "Oh, come on! Do I have to?" She said, "You certainly do! Don't talk back to me. How dare you!" I got mad and threw my books down and walked out of the room, slamming the door.

YOU: _____

BOB: I don't know why I did that. I just lost my temper.

YOU: What did the principal say?

BOB: She said she was surprised because I was usually a well-behaved student.

YOU: What's going to happen now?

BOB: I have to go to detention tomorrow.

YOU: _____

BOB: Yeah. I know I got off easy, but what am I going to tell my parents?

YOU: _____

BOB: I'll just tell them the truth. Boy, are they going to be mad!

YOU: _____

BOB: Thanks.

5. Anne has just gotten her report card. She has received an F in English.

You: What's wrong, Anne? You look blue.

ANNE: I failed English.

You: (show sympathy) _____

ANNE: My parents are going to kill me.

You: (show concern) _____

ANNE: What am I going to do?

You: _____

ANNE: I guess I'll just have to take my punishment.

You: _____

ANNE: _____

6. Sandy has received a present from her father. In the United States, people are expected to thank the giver for the gift, even if it is something the receiver doesn't want.

You: _____

SANDY: I feel so ungrateful. My father brought me a present when he came back from a business trip and I didn't even thank him. He got angry, and he was right.

You: _____

SANDY: He told me I was ungrateful and that I thought I had everything coming to me.

You: _____

SANDY: I know he didn't mean it, but I should have thanked him.

Idioms and Expressions from the Dialogues

Did you know what they meant? Could you figure them out from the context (the words around them and the meanings of the dialogues)?

to be laid off	to lose one's job until business at the company improves
to lose one's temper	to get angry
to be well behaved	to act properly, use good manners
to go to detention	to be kept at school as a means of punishment
to get a pass	to obtain from a teacher or principal a form that indicates that you have permission to do something

to talk back	to be impolite by saying something rude to an adult when no answer is necessary
How dare you!	an expression of surprise at someone's rudeness
to be blue	to feel sad or depressed
to have everything coming to you	to expect that you are entitled to have whatever you want and that you need not do anything in return

LET'S SHARE

Do people in your country talk to friends about their problems? What kinds of problems might each of these people discuss? With whom would they talk about their problems?

Person	Problems	Person with Whom to Talk
1. A teenager		
2. A young mother		
3. A 50-year-old man		
4. A 50-year-old woman		
5. A child		

5 PROBLEM SITUATIONS

Sometimes you will find yourself in a situation that requires that you act contrary to what your friends want or believe is correct. These situations are often difficult to handle. To find the answer, analyze the situation, decide how strongly you feel about it, and then act.

QUICK CUSTOMS QUIZ

Below are situations in which you might find yourself in the United States. Read each situation, decide what is appropriate, and choose the answer that best fits the circumstance. Draw a circle around the letter in front of your answer. Check your answers against those on page 162, which are the answers an American would probably give. When you have checked your answers, discuss them with your class. Then role-play each situation with another member of your class.

1. Your neighbor is playing his stereo very loudly. It is 3 o'clock in the morning and the music is preventing you from sleeping. What should you do?

   a. Shout for him to turn it down.
   b. Bang on the wall.
   c. Call him on the telephone and politely ask him to turn it down.
   d. Do nothing. He can do what he wants—it's a free country.
   e. Call the police.
   f. Call the landlord.
   g. Play your stereo just as loud.

2. At a party, your friend offers you marijuana or cocaine. When you politely refuse, he says, "Aw, come on! Everyone does it!" How should you handle this situation?

   a. Give him a lecture on using drugs.
   b. Say, "Thanks, but I'd rather not."
   c. Say, "Nobody but a real fool would use drugs, and you're obviously a fool." Then walk away.
   d. Ask him if his parents know that he is using drugs.
   e. Accept the drugs so that you will be accepted as a friend.

3. You are an excellent student and carefully prepare your homework every night. Your friend is having trouble in a class and asks to copy your work. What should you do?

   a. Let him copy your work.
   b. Help him by showing him how to do the homework but not by letting him copy your work.
   c. Refuse.
   d. Tell your professor.

4. You were assigned a roommate at your college. After living with that person for several weeks, you do not wish to live with him anymore. He is rude, messy, noisy, and inconsiderate. What should you do?

   a. Be rude, messy, noisy, and inconsiderate.
   b. Ask the housing authorities for another room and move out.
   c. Make his life miserable so that he will ask for another room and move out.
   d. Nothing. It will be too embarrassing to admit that you can't get along with your roommate.
   e. Tell him how you feel and work out a solution with him.

5. You have recently come to the United States and don't know many people. When you tell a friend that you would like to meet someone of the opposite sex, your friend offers to "fix you up with a blind date." What does he mean by this?

   a. He wants to introduce you to someone you don't know and have you go with this person on a date.
   b. He thinks that there is something wrong with you and wants you to go out with someone who can't see.
   c. He wants you to go on a date with someone who can't see.
   d. He wants you to go to a party where the lights are extremely dim.

NOW YOU DO IT

With a partner, choose one item from each question and develop a dialogue. After the instructor checks your dialogue, role-play it for the class.

1. Choose a happy situation from one of those below or add one of your own.

   a. You have just become an aunt or an uncle.
   b. You received an A on an English essay.
   c. You have been offered a job at which you will be earning $15 per hour.
   d. You meet a friend you haven't seen in ten years.

2. Choose a tense situation from the list that follows. Write a dialogue in which a friend uses conversational skills to find out what is wrong and then must be helpful and reassuring.

   a. You are worried about failing math.
   b. Your family hasn't written or called in a long time.
   c. Your 16-year-old sister wants to get married.
   d. You lost your job.
   e. You lost $50 from your wallet.
   f. The immigration officer wants to see you.

3. Choose one of the awkward situations below.

   a. Explain to your friend that he cannot bring his dog to the picnic with him.

b. Your friend has introduced you to a friend of his and hopes that you will like each other. You go on a "blind date" and find that you cannot get along. Tell your friend this in a nice way.

c. You are living with a person who will not do his or her part of the housework. Convince this person to do the dishes since you have done the cooking for the evening and it is his or her turn to clean up.

d. Drinking is against your religion; however, at a party, someone offers you a drink. This person does not mean to insult you. Refuse in a polite way.

four

Dating

In the United States, individuals have great freedom and opportunity to meet others. People from other countries are sometimes shocked to see what Americans do and say. They often go on dates in their early teens without a chaperone, share expenses on dates, and even live together without being married. From what one sees on television and in the movies, one might be led to believe that "anything goes." This is not the case, however, because Americans have rules for dating and relationships, even if they don't seem apparent. In this chapter, we will discuss the American concept of dating. You will have the opportunity to compare these concepts with those of your country.

1 DATING ACROSS CULTURES

Relationships between men and women, boys and girls are different all over the world. In some countries, families arrange a marriage before the bride and groom have met; in other countries, the young people select their own male and female friends, go on dates, and then tell their families whom they wish to marry.

LET'S SHARE

Look at the items listed here that define the relationship between males and females in the United States. Indicate whether this practice is the same or different in your country. If it is different, explain your custom.

In the United States	In Your Culture
Girls and boys of all ages go to school together.	
Boys and girls go to parties together.	
In colleges, some dormitories are coed (boys and girls live on the same floor but not in the same room).	
Starting at around the age of 14, girls and boys go on dates to the movies, dances, bowling, parties, roller skating, etc.	
If a couple gets a divorce, either or both persons may request custody of their children. The judge then decides which parent is best suited to care for the children, the father or the mother.	
Teenagers generally date people of their own age, although girls sometimes date boys two or three years older than they are.	
Girls may invite boys to parties or other social functions.	
Parents seldom play a role in selecting dates for their children.	

Box continued on following page

Box continued from preceding page

In the United States	In Your Culture
People of different social, economic, ethnic, or religious backgrounds sometimes date each other.	
Teenagers and adults select and meet their own dates.	
Most teenagers and unmarried adults go on dates with more than one person. They may go out with one person one week and someone else the next.	
In junior and senior high school, students often "pair up" with someone of the opposite sex.	
At the age of 18, many young people (men and women) live apart from their families, either at college or in their own apartment.	
Men and women who love each other sometimes live together without being married.	
Transportation is often provided by the person who asks for the date.	
Teenagers meet members of the opposite sex at school, parties, and other social functions.	

Box continued on following page

Box continued from preceding page

In the United States	*In Your Culture*
"Blind dates" are common.	
Sometimes men and women or boys and girls share expenses on a date.	
A boy usually picks up his date at her house.	

IDIOMS AND EXPRESSIONS

These idioms and expressions will help you understand the dating scene in the United States. See how many you know by matching the idioms and expressions with their definitions. Check your answers on page 162.

1. double date
2. to share expenses
3. blind date
4. to make a pass
5. to go steady; to be going with someone
6. to feed someone a line
7. to make out
8. to have an affair
9. to get picked up
10. a singles bar
11. to be stood up
12. to be seeing someone
13. to go stag
14. wallflower

A. to go somewhere without bringing a date
B. to form a sexual relationship
C. a girl who is not asked to dance and who stands around at the sidelines watching others
D. to meet someone (usually with sexual intent) without having been formally introduced
E. to be dating someone on a regular or exclusive basis
F. for each to pay his or her own way
G. a place where unmarried people go to meet each other
H. a date on which two couples go out together
I. to go out with only one special person
J. to mislead someone, especially in the interest of convincing that person to have a sexual relationship
K. to kiss passionately
L. a date arranged by a third party in which the other two have not met
M. to make sexual advances toward a person (usually by a man toward a woman), either to flatter her or to take advantage of her
N. to have one's date fail to appear or even send notice at the appointed time

Sometimes when people visit another country, they are surprised by what appears to be a lack of rules. This feeling is particularly noticeable when one tries to understand the relationships between men and women.

QUICK CUSTOMS QUIZ

Below are situations in which you might find yourself in the United States. Read each situation, decide what is appropriate, and choose the answer that best fits the circumstance. Draw a circle around the letter in front of your answer. Check your answers against those on page 163, which are the answers an American would probably give. (There may be more than one correct answer.)

1. You are a young woman at a party. A man across the room catches your eye and smiles. You think he looks pleasant, and you would like to meet him. What should you do?

    a. Turn your eyes away.
    b. Go to a group of your friends and ignore him.
    c. Smile.
    d. Get angry because he is so rude.

2. You are a young man in a cafeteria at school. You see a young woman you would like to meet. What should you do?

    a. Make noises and follow her.
    b. Go up to her and tell her she is beautiful.
    c. Pinch her.
    d. Nothing.
    e. Catch her eye and smile.

3. You are a young woman on a date. Your date says, "Let's go to my place." What does this usually mean?

    a. He wants you to go to his apartment and have sex with him.
    b. He wants you to meet his parents.
    c. He is very proud of his apartment and wants to show it to you.

4. You have gone out with someone four or five times and you like this person very much. What touching in public is acceptable?

    a. None.
    b. Holding hands.
    c. The man may put his arm around the woman's shoulder or waist.
    d. Kissing hello and good-bye on the lips.
    e. Passionate kissing.

5. Where do people usually go on a date?

   a. the movies
   b. dinner
   c. for dessert or a light snack
   d. bowling
   e. the beach
   f. party
   g. theater
   h. roller skating
   i. sporting events

6. When you go on a date, should you bring your date a present?

   a. Yes.
   b. Only if it is a special occasion such as a prom.

7. If a man asks a woman to go to the movies or to dinner, who should pay?

   a. They should split the bill.
   b. The woman should pay.
   c. The man should pay.

8. When arrangements are made to go on a date, where does the couple usually meet?

   a. They meet at the restaurant or theater.
   b. The man picks up the woman at her home.

MODEL DIALOGUES

Here are some conversation models in which people invite someone of the opposite sex to go out on a date or to a party. Practice these models with a classmate.

1. JIM: Hi, Susan.
   SUSAN: Hi, Jim.
   JIM: I was wondering if you are doing something Friday night. I have tickets to a rock concert.
   SUSAN: Which one?
   JIM: I have two tickets to see the Flaming Idiots concert. Would you like to go with me?
   SUSAN: I'd love to!
   JIM: Great! I'll pick you up at seven o'clock.
   SUSAN: OK. See you then.
   JIM: Good-bye.

2. LAURIE: Hi, Jeff.
   JEFF: Hello. How's it going?

LAURIE: Great. I'm having a party Saturday night and I'd like you to come.

JEFF: Thanks. What time does it start?

LAURIE: Eight-thirty. Can you come?

JEFF: Sure, I wouldn't miss one of your parties.

3. JULIE: Hi, Alex.

ALEX: Oh, Julie. You're just the person I wanted to see!

JULIE: Really? What's up?

ALEX: How would you like to go to next Saturday's football game with me?

JULIE: Next Saturday? Gee, I'm sorry. I can't. That's my mother's birthday.

ALEX: Oh, I was really hoping that you could go.

JULIE: Well, maybe some other time.

The third conversation is particularly important because the person who is being invited has declined the invitation politely. Julie has given a good reason for saying that she can't go to the game and is letting Alex know that perhaps she would be interested in going with him at another time.

There are two other ways in which she could have handled the situation, however. If she really did want to go out with Alex and wanted to express her interest strongly, she could have declined in this manner:

ALEX: Oh, I was really hoping you could go.

JULIE: Yes, me, too. *How about the game on the following Saturday?*

ALEX: That's a great idea! I'll call you later in the week and we can decide on when to go and what to do after the game.

Julie makes her willingness clear by suggesting an alternative. Sometimes you really don't want to date a person but wish to avoid hurting that person's feelings. Let's consider how Julie could have handled the situation if she did not want to go on a date with Alex:

ALEX: Oh, I was really hoping you could go.

JULIE: *Thank you for asking me anyway.*

Here Julie politely declines the invitation and thanks Alex for asking her but does not indicate that she would like to go out at another time.

NOW YOU DO IT

In groups of three, write a dialogue for the following situations. Take turns having two people role-playing the situation and one student observing and commenting on how they handled the situation.

1. You wish to ask someone to your party on Saturday. After the other person accepts, you provide details about when and where it will be held and who will be attending.

2. Someone asks you on a date. You do not wish to go but don't wish to hurt this person's feelings. You do not wish to have this person ask you out again.
3. You have been asked to a party and cannot attend because you must baby-sit. Decline but let the other person know that you would like to be invited some other time.
4. You and your friend have decided to spend Saturday evening together. Decide where you will go, what you'll do, and when you'll meet.
5. Someone you like has invited you to go to the drive-in, an outdoor movie that you watch from your car. You prefer to go to movies in an indoor theater. Discuss this with your date and suggest going to another theater.

3 COMPLIMENTS AND CONVERSATION

Now that you have made arrangements to go out, what will you talk about on your date? Most people begin with small talk such as the weather and then move on to areas of mutual interest. It is common to compliment one's date. Here are some ways to give and to accept compliments.

1. TED: Hi. You look great!
   KATHY: Thank you, Ted.

2. LISA: That's a nice jacket, Bob.
   BOB: Thanks. I bought it just for this occasion.

3. CYNTHIA: I like your tie. Is it new?
   JERRY: Yes, thank you. I got it for my birthday.

NOW YOU DO IT

If the dating customs in your country are different from those practiced in the United States, you may want to talk about these differences with your date. In the following conversation, an international student is on a blind date. As a topic of conversation, he mentions that blind dates do not take place in his country. That leads to a conversation about dating customs and other areas of discussion. Complete this conversation as you would if you were the person on the blind date. Then role-play it with a class member.

YOU: This is my first blind date. We don't do this in my country.
DATE: What do you do to meet people?
YOU: _____
DATE: That's very interesting. But what if _____?
YOU: _____

DATE: Do you have singles bars or dating services?
YOU: _____
DATE: How old are people when they begin to go out on dates in your country?
YOU: _____
DATE: What kinds of things do people do on dates?
YOU: _____
DATE: Your country sounds like an interesting place. I'd like to visit there sometime. What do you think that I should do when I go to your country?
YOU: _____
DATE: America seems very different from _____. Are there any customs that I should know before I get there so that I won't offend someone?
YOU: _____
DATE: That's good to know! I'd never have thought of that.
YOU: Well, are you ready to go to the movie now?
DATE: _____

When the date is over, it is customary for the man to take the woman home. She thanks him for an enjoyable evening. Sometimes on a first date, a couple, if they like each other, may kiss good night.

SUE: Thank you for a lovely evening.
JOE: I had a great time, too. I'll call you this week and perhaps we can go out again next weekend.
SUE: Yes, I'd like that. Good night, Joe.
JOE: (*leans over and kisses her*) Good night, Sue.

Notice that in this conversation, Joe indicates that he would like to date Susan again, and she agrees.

ROLE PLAY

Form groups of three or four people. Discuss how you would handle each of the following situations. Then take turns acting out the situations while other group members observe. The observers should notice the body language and facial expressions of the actors as well as their words.

1. You wish to ask someone on a date to go to the football game at the local college. Choose a partner and make arrangements. (The other person may accept or refuse.)
2. You are a young woman who is at a party alone. A young man comes up to you and makes a pass. Handle the situation tactfully.
3. You are at a party and see someone you would like to meet. Find and role-play two ways of meeting this person. After you meet, carry on small talk for three minutes.
4. You don't know anyone in town and tell a friend that you would like to meet someone nice to go out with. Your friend tells you that he has arranged a blind date for you. Role-play the situation as you obtain all the important details.

5. You are a woman who has had a lovely evening with your date, but on the way to take you home, he suggests that you "go back to his place." Handle this situation tactfully by either agreeing or refusing. Remember that you wish to keep his friendship and his respect.

6. You are a man on a date with a young woman whom you don't know well. During the evening, you have held hands and kissed several times. However, at the end of the evening, she suggests that you "come back to her apartment." Handle this situation tactfully either by refusing or agreeing. Remember that you wish to keep her friendship and her respect.

Sharing Common Interests

International students are often surprised at American attitudes toward humor, animals, and superstitions. For example, one student who was living with an American family was shocked at how they treated the family dog. "I couldn't believe it," he said. "The dog had a bed in the child's room and was actually allowed to sit on the living room sofa. The dog even had his own food in cans, which is very expensive. Worse than that, they fed the dog right from the dining room table!"

American humor also seems strange at times. For instance, Americans enjoy making jokes about politicians and government policies. They even print "bumper stickers" that feature funny sayings about their attitudes and occupations, such as "Nurses Are Patient People."

Although the United States is supposed to be very modern, it also has its share of superstitions, many of which are common to other cultures.

Along with many other areas like gardening, sports, finances, and art, humor, superstition, and pets form common interests that are shared among friends.

1 AMERICAN HUMOR

Humor is universal; however, each culture finds different things funny. If you have ever tried to translate a joke from your native language into another language for someone, you probably were disappointed because your listener may not have thought it was funny. Something was literally "lost in the translation."

Let's try an experiment. Think of a joke that people in your culture find funny. Translate it into English, and write it on the lines below.

_____

_____

_____

_____

_____

_____

_____

Now share your joke with someone from another culture. Does that person think it's funny?

RIDDLES

Like gestures, humor varies from one culture to another. In the United States, children often enjoy telling riddles. A riddle is a question that is hard to answer because it involves some kind of trick such as a play on words.

See if you can solve the following riddles. The answers are on page 163. After you check your answer, discuss the trick that made each riddle difficult to answer.

1. What has four wheels and flies? _____
2. What has four legs and no head? _____
3. What begins with "T," ends with "T," and has "T" in the middle? _____
4. What is black and white and "read" all over? _____
5. What would you have if you painted every automobile in the United States pink? _____

LET'S SHARE

Write a riddle that children in your country enjoy. Share it with the class.

_____

_____

_____

_____

KNOCK-KNOCK JOKES

Children also enjoy "knock-knock" jokes like these. One person pretends to be knocking at the door, and the other one pretends to answer.

ANN: Knock! Knock!
MARY: Who's there?
ANN: Ida.
MARY: Ida who?
ANN: Ida Wanna. (*Ida Wanna* sounds like "I don't want to.")

TERESA: Knock! Knock!
MARTY: Who's there?
TERESA: Orange.
MARTY: Orange who?
TERESA: Orange you glad I'm your friend? (*Orange you* sounds like "aren't you.")

Notice that certain parts of the joke are always the same:

PERSON: *Knock! Knock!*
YOU: *Who's there?*
PERSON: Boo.
YOU: Boo *who?*
PERSON: Why are you crying?

NOW YOU DO IT

Try each of these jokes with a partner.

1. YOU: Knock! Knock!
   PARTNER: Who's there?
   YOU: Robert.
   PARTNER: Robert who?
   YOU: You mean you don't know either?

2. YOU: Knock! Knock!
   PARTNER: Who's there?
   YOU: Adam.
   PARTNER: Adam who?
   YOU: Adam up and give me the bill. (Sounds like "add 'em up.")

3. YOU: Knock! Knock!
   PARTNER: Who's there?
   YOU: Sofa.
   PARTNER: Sofa who?
   YOU: Sofa you're doing fine! (Sounds like "so far.")

4. Now try making up one of your own!
   YOU: Knock! Knock!
   PARTNER: Who's there?
   YOU: _____
   PARTNER: _____
   YOU: _____

ANALYSIS

Americans value the ability to laugh at oneself and others. They enjoy jokes which make fun of professions like doctors, lawyers, and politicians. They also like ethnic jokes and jokes about mothers-in-law, wives, husbands, religion, and sex. Here are some examples of jokes. Try to figure them out before you read the explanations.

1. A doctor, a priest, and a lawyer found themselves stranded in the ocean. After their boat tipped over, a shark appeared and promptly ate the doctor and the priest. Then he carried the lawyer on his back to safety. The lawyer was very surprised and asked the shark why he had killed the others but spared his life. The shark replied, "Professional courtesy."
   Can you explain the meaning?
2. A doctor told his patient that he needed surgery immediately. The cost of the operation was $12,000, but the patient could pay it off at the rate of $300 per month. "My goodness," replied the patient, "That's as much as buying a car!" "Yes," said the doctor, "I am."
   Can you explain the meaning?
3. My son had the car out on Sunday and hit a tree. He insists it wasn't his fault because he blew the horn.
   Can you explain the meaning?

Meanings

1. A shark is a dangerous, man-eating fish. Some people see lawyers who charge large fees for their services as being like sharks. Professional courtesy is when people of the same or similar professions don't charge each other for their services.
2. The doctor is buying a new car and has set up his fees to cover his car payments.
3. The stereotype of American teenagers is that they are always right. In this case, the teenager insists he was on the right because he blew the horn; the tree should have moved.

Americans also enjoy humor that employs words with more than one meaning. Each of the words listed below has more than one meaning. Use a dictionary to find two different meanings for each word.

Word	First Meaning	Second Meaning
Patient		
Swingers		

Box continued on following page

Box continued from preceding page

Word	First Meaning	Second Meaning
Class		
Pull		
Kick		

Now look at the one-liners below. Can you explain their humor (double meanings)?

Nurses are patient people.
Tennis is for swingers.
Teachers have class.
Voters have pull.
Soccer players get a kick out of life.

LET'S SHARE

Sayings like the ones just listed and the ones that follow are often found on T-shirts, bumper stickers, and buttons in the United States.

Saying	Meaning
Bald is beautiful.	Usually baldness is seen as negative. However, each person should be valued for what he is.
If you can read this, thank a teacher.	Teachers don't get enough recognition for the contribution they make.

What sayings do people in your country use? List them here with their meaning.

72

Saying	Meaning

2 SUPERSTITIONS

Each culture has its own superstitions. Superstitions are beliefs that are not founded on scientific proof but nevertheless persist from generation to generation. Listed here are a number of superstitions people in the United States may have.

Superstition	Meaning
Breaking a mirror	You will have seven years of bad luck.
Walking under a ladder	You will have bad luck.
Finding a four-leaf clover	You will have good luck.
A black cat's crossing your path	You will have bad luck.
The number 13	This is a very unlucky number. This superstition is so widely believed that many buildings do not have a thirteenth floor.
Knocking on wood	When you receive a compliment about yourself or a loved one or tell about something fortunate that has happened, you should "knock on wood" to prevent something bad from happening.
Crossing one's fingers	You wish to have good luck.

LET'S SHARE

1. Divide into small groups and compile a list of superstitions from your countries. One person from each group should be prepared to share that group's list with the class.

_____

_____

_____

_____

2. In the United States, a holiday based on superstition is Halloween. This holiday is based on the belief that the souls of the dead, especially the evil ones, walk the earth on October 31. On this day, children dress up in scary costumes and go from house to house shouting, "Trick or treat." People give children candy or prizes so that the children will not play a "trick," such as putting soap on their windows. Of course, Americans no longer believe in evil spirits and witches but enjoy the holiday as a day of fun for children.

   Does your culture have a day that is surrounded by superstition? Tell your group or the class about this day and where the superstition came from.

3. Why do you think people are superstitious? Are people growing more or less superstitious? Why?

NOW YOU DO IT

Now that we have discussed superstitions, complete each of these conversations. Then role-play them with a partner.

1. You: Hi, Sue. How's everything?
   Sue: Fine. Have you had the flu? It's been going around?
   You: _____
   Sue: No one in my family has had it. We're all healthy, knock on wood.
   You: _____
   Sue: See you.

2. You: _____
   Janet: I have a social studies test next period. I'm really nervous. Cross your fingers for me, will you?
   You: _____
   Janet: Thanks a lot!

3. You: _____
   David: I just got a speeding ticket.
   You: _____

74

DAVID: Everything's gone wrong today! My alarm didn't go off and I was late for work. I couldn't find my keys, and now this. You'd think that today was Friday the thirteenth or something.

YOU: _____

DAVID: See you later!

3 PETS

Most Americans have pets. Pets can be dogs or cats, gerbils, hamsters, mice, guinea pigs, parakeets, canaries, or tropical fish. Pets usually live in the house and are treated with great care and affection. Dogs and cats generally have the freedom to walk around in the house, and their food is usually kept on the floor in the kitchen. It is not unusual for pets to be fed food from the family table.

LET'S SHARE

Are pets kept in your country? What kinds of pets are popular? Do they live in the house or outdoors? Do people feel the same way about pets in your country as they do in the United States?

Form small groups and discuss differences and similarities. When you have finished your discussion, have one person present your group's findings to the class.

NOW YOU DO IT

Here is a series of conversations about pets that you might hear in the United States. Complete each conversation. Then role-play it with a partner.

1. You meet a friend who is walking a small black-and-white puppy.

YOU: What a cute puppy!
FRIEND: _____
YOU: How old is he?
FRIEND: _____
YOU: _____
FRIEND: He is a rat terrier, a very rare dog now because most people are interested in larger dogs for protection.

2. You ring the doorbell of your friend's house, and a dog starts barking.

FRIEND: Hi. Come on in.
YOU: _____

FRIEND: Oh, don't worry. He won't hurt you.
YOU: _____
FRIEND: Would you like me to put him in another room while you're
         here?
YOU: _____

3. You are visiting a friend's house and notice that he has a large aquarium in his living room.

YOU: What pretty fish!
FRIEND: Thank you. I really enjoy keeping them.
YOU: _____
FRIEND: These are guppies, and the black ones are mollies.
YOU: _____
FRIEND: About a year now, but I had fish when I was a small child.

PETS IN AMERICA

Here is a list of facts about pets in the United States.

1. Americans spend a great deal of money on their pets every year. Some even buy coats and fancy collars for their dogs and cats.
2. It is against the law in the United States to mistreat an animal. A person could have to pay a large fine or even go to jail if convicted.
3. The cost of pet care is so high that insurance companies are beginning to sell health insurance for pets.
4. People sometimes bury their pets in very expensive pet cemeteries. These cemeteries sometimes allow the owner to be buried beside the pet, just as parents and children are buried near each other in other cemeteries. Sometimes people buy large, stone headstones for their pet's grave.
5. Some dogs and cats are fed directly from the table and are given beds and pillows in the house. They are treated "like one of the family."

Choose one of the statements on this list. After you have carefully organized your thoughts, tell your classmates how you feel about the statement. Then tell how people in your country treat pets.

six

Participating in Social Events

eligious customs and social events are central to any nationality. They provide the means to deal with birth, marriage, and death. These events are also the stepping-stones to adulthood and acceptance in the community. In this chapter, we will discuss various social events, ways to deal with difficult social situations, and conversations appropriate in each. As you work through this chapter, be sure to apply what you have learned and discussed in earlier chapters so that you can sharpen your speaking skills and gain a deeper understanding of American culture.

PHOTO ESSAY

Can you tell what is happening in these photographs? What function is taking place? See the answers on the bottom of page 78.

A

B

C

Photo identifications: (A) a child's birthday party; (B) a wedding; (C) a funeral.

1 SOCIAL EVENTS

LET'S SHARE

Here is a chart of important social events and ways that they are observed in the United States. After you discuss these American customs with your class, write how you observe these occasions in your culture.

Event	Celebration in the United States	Celebration in Your Country
Birth	Friends give a baby shower for expectant mother; gift for baby; flowers for mother in the hospital; send birth announcement to friends; send greeting cards to new parents	
Birthday	Adults celebrate with family and usually have a cake with candles; children have parties, invite friends, wear hats, play games, receive prizes, eat cake and ice cream; guests bring relatively inexpensive presents	
Marriage	*Engagement:* Fiancé gives future wife a ring, usually with a diamond; bride's friends give bridal showers where bride receives household gifts; friends of the groom give him a "stag party." *Wedding:* Guests attend the ceremony and, if invited, a reception afterwards; guests give gifts, usually of expensive silver, china or glassware, or money.	
Wedding anniversary	Husband and wife spend the evening together or go out with friends. On twenty-fifth and fiftieth wedding anniversary, family and friends give the couple a special party and bring them presents.	
Death	*Funeral home:* Friends gather at the funeral home or chapel to pay their respects, offer condolences; they send flowers or make a contribution to a charity in the name of the deceased. *Funeral:* Family and close friends go to the religious service and then to the cemetery to pay their respects.	

ANALYSIS

After examining the pictures at the start of this chapter, fill in the chart describing the type of clothing worn at each event. Then fill out the chart describing the clothes worn in your country. When you have finished, share this information with your classmates.

Event	Dress in the United States	Dress in Your Country
Birthday party for children		
Wedding ceremony		
Funeral		

2 SAYING THE RIGHT THING AT WEDDINGS AND FUNERALS

Conversationally and emotionally, weddings and funerals are two of the most difficult events to attend. Although weddings are festive, happy times, guests often know few people and therefore must have sharp conversational skills, especially for small talk. Funerals are even more difficult because one wants to say something consoling to the family of the deceased but often cannot find the words. This section provides a guide for conversation in these events that you can shape to your own needs and feelings.

ATTENDING A WEDDING: APPROPRIATE CONVERSATION

Weddings are festive times in the United States. The two families plan the wedding and reception together, although the bride's family generally pays for the wedding. Usually the bride wears a long white gown and veil to signify purity, and the groom and his attendants wear tuxedos. Guests generally wear dressy clothes to the service and reception.

The reception is a party for the bride and groom after the wedding service to which one must be invited. At the reception, there is a receiving line made up of the bride and groom and their families. Guests pass from person to person in the receiving line to give their congratulations and good wishes.

Gifts are either sent to the bride's house before the wedding or brought to the reception.

Small talk, as you learned in Chapter Two, is light conversation about general subjects such as the weather. Small talk is particularly useful when you don't know the other person well and wish to begin a conversation. This type of conversation usually lasts only a few minutes. Here are some of the types of small talk people engage in at different times at a wedding.

Model Dialogues

YOU: What a handsome couple they make.
ACQUAINTANCE: Yes, isn't she a lovely bride!
YOU: Do you know where they plan to honeymoon?
ACQUAINTANCE: Yes. I believe they are going to Niagara Falls.
YOU: That's a popular honeymoon spot in the United States, isn't it?
ACQUAINTANCE: Yes. Where are you from?
YOU: I'm from Nigeria.
ACQUAINTANCE: Where do people in your country honeymoon?

This is an example of a conversation that might take place in a receiving line at a wedding:

ACQUAINTANCE: Which side of the family are you with?
YOU: I'm a friend of the bride.
ACQUAINTANCE: Oh. I'm the groom's uncle, Jim Martin.
YOU: Nice to meet you. I'm Barbara Fields.
ACQUAINTANCE: How do you know the bride?
YOU: We went to high school together.

ATTENDING A FUNERAL: APPROPRIATE CONVERSATION

In the United States, people are of several religions. The predominant religions are Catholic, Protestant, and Jewish. Each handles death in a different way. In the Protestant and Catholic religions, religious services are held at a church; in the Jewish religion, at a synagogue. In addition to attending the religious service, people may go to a funeral home to express their sympathy to the grieving family. In the Jewish religion, people may go to the funeral home to express sympathy and may also pay a visit to the grieving family during the next week. At this time, the family is "sitting shiva" at the home of one of its members.

When attending a funeral, clothes should be simple, in either dark or neutral shades. In the South and among Jews, it is customary to return to the house of the deceased for a light lunch if one is a close friend of the family. The food is provided by friends of the family and may be anything from desserts to a meat dish.

81

Although most Americans send flowers, they also make contributions to charities in the deceased's name, especially if requested by the family to do so instead of sending flowers. The obituary notice in the newspaper will state the charity to which they wish the donations to be sent.

Model Dialogues

Here are some samples of conversations one might hear to express sympathy.

1. YOU: He (she) certainly was a wonderful person.
   BEREAVED PERSON: Yes. We will miss him (her) very much.

2. BEREAVED PERSON: I just spoke to him (her) last week.
   YOU: He (she) was very special to me. I remember when . . . (*tell incident*)

3. YOU: I'm sorry about your loss.
   BEREAVED PERSON: I will miss him (her) so much.
   YOU: I know. It's a very sad time.

4. Sometimes we don't know people well enough to attend the funeral but still wish to express sympathy.
   YOU: I was sorry to hear about your (mother, father, sister, brother, husband, wife, child, friend).
   FRIEND: Thank you.

NOW YOU DO IT

1. In groups of three, take turns role-playing these situations. Make sure that you use appropriate body language and gestures. The person who is watching the role play should evaluate how the other two students handle each situation.

   a. Tell the mother of the bride how lovely her daughter looks and that you wish the couple happiness.
   b. You meet a friend at a wedding and talk about the bride or groom. You may talk about where she or he lives or goes to school, how long they have known each other, where they met, etc.
   c. Your close friend has died. Express your sympathy to your friend's brother or sister.
   d. Your teacher's father, whom you don't know, has died. Express your sympathy.

2. Be prepared to discuss with your class how funeral and wedding customs are different in your country. Choose one event from either the wedding or the funeral and discuss its significance.

Holidays often represent religious or patriotic events that most of the people in a country share in celebrating. In many countries, there is a state religion. The government and the religious leaders may work together to set political policies and decide on government actions.

In the United States, however, people believe in the separation of church and state. This means that the government may not interfere with or support matters relating to religion and religious institutions may not interfere in matters of government.

Because people living in the United States come from all over the world, they have learned to enjoy holidays that are part of other people's cultures but not their own and to respect people's right to worship in their own way. For example, most Americans, Christian or not, enjoy attending Christmas parties. They may also wear the customary green on St. Patrick's Day even though they are not all Irish.

AMERICAN HOLIDAYS

Here is a list of American holidays, when they are celebrated, and some information about how they are celebrated.

Holiday	Time of Year	Type of Celebration
New Year's Eve	Evening of December 31	People dress up to go out to dinner, movies, theater, or parties. Most parties begin at 9 or 10 P.M.
New Year's Day	January 1	People relax from previous evening's festivities. They may visit with friends. Many watch college football games on television.
Dr. Martin Luther King's Birthday	January 15	Some schools and businesses close in honor of this slain civil rights leader.
Valentine's Day	February 14	Children exchange greeting cards in school. Sweethearts exchange cards. Men give flowers or candy to the women they love (wife, daughter, mother, girlfriend).
Presidents' Day (Combined celebration of Washington's Birthday and Lincoln's Birthday)	Third Monday in February	Many schools close for one week vacation. Banks and the post office close for the day.
St. Patrick's Day	March 17	Irish holiday, celebrated with parades. People wear green.
April Fool's Day	April 1	A day when people, especially children, like to play tricks on others.

Box continued on following page

Box continued from preceding page

Holiday	Time of Year	Type of Celebration
Passover	Eight days in the spring	Jewish religious holiday celebrating Jews' escape from slavery in Egypt. On the first two nights, Jewish people have a traditional family meal called a seder.
Easter	A Sunday in the spring	Christian religious holiday. Some people stay home from work or school on the preceding Friday (Good Friday). On Easter Sunday, Christian families attend church and gather for traditional meals. (In addition, many Americans enjoy buying chocolate Easter bunnies, candy eggs, and jelly beans. There are Easter egg hunts, and children color Easter eggs.)
Mother's Day	First Sunday in May	The extended family gathers; mothers and grandmothers receive cards and gifts.
Memorial Day	Last Monday in May	A day honoring all who have died in war. Schools and all government offices and businesses are closed.
Father's Day	Third Sunday in June	Families gather; fathers and grandfathers receive cards and gifts.
Independence Day	July 4	The day that the United States declared independence from England is celebrated with parades, picnics, barbecues, and fireworks.
Labor Day	First Monday in September	The final summer vacation day before school begins. People go to picnics and have outdoor parties with family and friends.
Rosh Hashanah	Two days in the fall	Jewish New Year, celebrated by going to synagogue.
Yom Kippur	Tenth day following Rosh Hashanah	Day of Atonement in the Jewish religion; Jews fast and go to synagogue.
Columbus Day	October 12	The day Christopher Columbus discovered America. Schools, banks, and post offices are closed.
Veterans' Day	Fourth Monday in October	A day honoring all people who have served in the armed forces; people display flags, and there are parades.
Halloween	October 31	Children dress up in costumes and go door to door saying "trick or treat". They expect people to give them candy.
Thanksgiving	Fourth Thursday in November	Commemorates the Pilgrims' first harvest in the New World. Celebrated with a large meal, traditionally roast turkey.

Box continued on following page

Box continued from preceding page

Holiday	Time of Year	Type of Celebration
Hanukkah	Eight days in late fall	The Jewish Festival of Lights; families light candles and exchange small gifts on each of the eight nights.
Christmas	December 25	Christian holiday celebrating the birth of Jesus Christ. Families gather to exchange gifts and eat a traditional meal. Families decorate Christmas trees with ornaments and sing songs. Santa Claus, a fat, jolly man in a white beard, brings gifts to all.

Analysis

Look at the photos and see if you can identify the holidays. Refer to the chart, if necessary. Check your answers on page 163.

A

B

C

D

E

GREETING CARDS

Greeting cards are a popular way that Americans have of expressing their feelings on a variety of occasions. Cards are printed not only for birthdays and anniversaries, Mother's Day and Father's Day, Christmas and New Year's but also for graduation, Valentine's Day, and many other events. People in the United States send get-well cards to people who are ill and even cards to express friendship. However, with the exception of Christmas cards, you should know someone well or see them often before sending them a card or buying them a gift. The only time it is appropriate to give a gift to someone you don't know well is if you are invited to a party to celebrate a birthday or an anniversary. Some business people send cards to clients to maintain good-will. Some people never send cards.

Matching

For what occasion would you buy the following greeting cards? Match the message inside the card with the event. Check your answers on page 164.

	Message		**Event**

_____ 1. Sorry to hear of your loss.

_____ 2. Another year, another gray hair.

_____ 3. May the bells always be ringing.

_____ 4. You two must have something very special.

_____ 5. Time goes by slowly when you're not here.

_____ 6. Writing doesn't seem to be one of your favorite pastimes, but I hope to hear from you soon.

_____ 7. Here's to another 50 years together.

_____ 8. May you soon be out of bed and back on the tennis courts.

Event

A. Wedding

B. Death

C. Birthday

D. Anniversary

E. Golden anniversary

F. Friendship

G. Love

H. Illness

LET'S SHARE

The chart below indicates who an American would send a birthday card to. Indicate with an **X** who you would send a greeting card to in your country.

Relationship	In the United States			In Your Country		
	Yes	No	Maybe	Yes	No	Maybe
1. Parents	X					
2. Neighbor			X			
3. Acquaintance		X				
4. Good friend	X					
5. Colleague			X			
6. Boyfriend	X					
7. Girlfriend	X					
8. Teacher		X				
9. Classmate			X			
10. Uncle/aunt	X					
11. Wife/husband	X					

Generally, in the United States, cards are sent only if one has established a warm relationship with the other person.

NOW YOU DO IT

Complete this practice dialogue. You wish to buy a card for your mother's birthday. Ask the salesperson to help you.

You: _____

Salesperson: Yes. The birthday cards are right over here.

You: _____

Salesperson: Are you looking for a particular kind of card? We have sentimental cards, humorous cards, and even cards that are written especially for mothers.

You: _____

Salesperson: That is an excellent choice. I hope she likes it.

You: _____

4 GOING OUT WITH FRIENDS

In the United States, there are many kinds of social events to take part in. Some events are casual and others are formal. However, they all offer challenges to guests in terms of what they should do and how they should respond to invitations.

MATCHING

Here are some terms used to describe social events or phrases that are used on invitations. Match them with the correct definition. The answers are on page 164.

_____ 1. B.Y.O.B.

_____ 2. R.S.V.P.

_____ 3. Regrets only

_____ 4. Cocktail party

_____ 5. Prom

_____ 6. Wedding reception

_____ 7. Wedding ceremony

A. A party at which guests play card games like bridge, euchre, poker, or gin (casual dress)

B. A party held at someone's home in the early afternoon or evening at which light refreshments are served (wear nice dress, suit)

C. Respond to the invitation only if you are *not* coming

_____ 8. Baby shower

_____ 9. Potluck dinner

_____ 10. Mixer

_____ 11. Open house

_____ 12. Surprise party

_____ 13. Card party

_____ 14. Graduation party

_____ 15. Picnic

_____ 16. Cookout

D. A party for an honored guest who is not told before the party

E. Please let the host know whether or not you intend to attend

F. A party for an expectant mother to which everyone brings a gift (women only—casual dress)

G. A party to introduce men and women (dress varies)

H. Bring your own bottle (if you wish to drink wine or liquor)

I. A dinner to which everyone brings a dish of food to share (casual dress)

J. A formal dance (wear tuxedo, evening dress) for a high school graduation

K. The ceremony at which two people are married

L. The party after a wedding (wear suit, nice dress)

M. A party at which light refreshments and alcoholic beverages are served (wear suit, nice dress)

N. A party to honor someone who has recently graduated from high school or college

O. An informal gathering at which meat is cooked over an open fire or outdoor grill and served with salads and potato chips

P. A packed lunch, usually consisting of sandwiches, fried chicken, potato or bean salad, and dessert, eaten in a park or open field

LET'S SHARE

What are some important social events in your country? How are they different from those in the United States? Give two examples and provide information so that a visitor to your country would know how to act and what to bring and wear to the social event.

Event	What Happens	Who Attends	What to Wear	When to Arrive
1.				
2.				

When you have finished, share the information with your class. Be prepared to answer questions and to give examples.

QUICK CUSTOMS QUIZ

Below are situations in which you might find yourself in the United States. Read each situation, decide what is appropriate, and choose the answer that best fits the circumstance. Draw a circle around the letter in front of your answer. Check your answers against those on page 164, which are the answers an American would probably give. (There may be more than one correct answer.)

1. You are invited to a friend's house for dinner. What should you bring?

    a. A bottle of wine
    b. Flowers for the hostess
    c. Nothing
    d. Some food to cook
    e. A friend or a relative
    f. Your children
    g. A gift costing more than $10

2. You are eating dinner at a friend's house or in a restaurant. Where should you keep your hands when you are not holding eating utensils?

a. In your lap
b. On the table
c. By your side

3. You are an adult who has been invited to an open house. What do you expect it to be like? Check all that apply.

a. The men talking in one room and the women in another
b. Men and women talking together
c. Everyone standing
d. Everyone sitting
e. Men and women drinking liquor
f. A quiet atmosphere
g. A noisy atmosphere

4. When you are eating with others around a table, which of the following should you do?

a. Carry on a conversation
b. Eat in silence
c. Make smacking noises and other eating noises to show that you are enjoying the meal
d. Burp to show that you enjoyed the meal
e. Chew with your mouth closed
f. Talk with food in your mouth

5. You are invited to a friend's home for dinner. After you eat the food you are served, you are still hungry and would enjoy more. What should you do?

a. Wait for the friend to ask you several times if you want "seconds" (a second helping of food)
b. Accept the friend's first offer of seconds and say, "Yes, thank you. It is delicious."
c. Help yourself
d. Don't eat any more because the host will think you are impolite or unable to get enough to eat at home

6. A friend says to you, "Let's go out to dinner sometime." What does he or she mean?

a. He or she will pay for both dinners.
b. You will pay for both dinners.
c. Each of you will pay for your own dinner.

7. When a friend says, "Why don't you come over and visit sometime," what does he or she mean?

a. You may go to this friend's house whenever you want.
b. Your friend is making pleasant conversation but is not inviting you to visit.

8. When a couple is led to a table in a restaurant, who should go first?

   a. The man
   b. The woman

9. You wish to attract the waiter's attention in a restaurant. What should you do?

   a. Snap your fingers
   b. Tap your glass with your spoon
   c. Catch the waiter's eye and raise your hand
   d. Whistle
   e. Shout out the waiter's name
   f. Call out, "Waiter" or "Sir"

10. You and your friend have ordered an alcoholic beverage at a disco, bar, or restaurant. Before he will serve you, the waiter asks to see your identification. What should you show him? (Check all that apply.)

    a. Your driver's license
    b. Your social security card
    c. Your passport
    d. Your school ID card
    e. Your cash or traveler's checks

11. The waiter has left your check on the table. How can you pay for it?

    a. Cash
    b. Personal check
    c. Credit card
    d. Money from your country
    e. Traveler's checks

12. There appears to be a $2.50 charge on your check for an item that you did not order. What should you do?

    a. Forget it. It's not worth the trouble.
    b. Get the waiter and tell him that there appears to be a mistake on your bill.
    c. Get angry and demand that the waiter correct the mistake immediately.
    d. Ask for the manager or headwaiter (also sometimes called the "maître d'").
    e. Pay the bill and when you get home, write a letter to the restaurant explaining the problem.

LET'S SHARE

When you checked your answers you may have been surprised at some of the answers to the Quick Customs Quiz because they are different from the actions that would be acceptable in your country. Choose two items that would be handled differently at home and explain how and why those actions would be appropriate. Then share your answers with the class.

1. Question _____

_____

_____

_____

_____

_____

2. Question _____

_____

_____

_____

_____

_____

5 THE CONCEPT OF TIME

You are invited to a friend's house for dinner at 6 P.M. What time should you arrive?

a. 5:30 P.M.   b. 6:00 P.M.   c. 7:00 P.M.

These are the reactions you might get if you arrived at these times:

5:30 P.M.   6:00 P.M.   7:00 P.M.

In the United States, time is exact. People plan activities and arrange their lives around specific times. For example, in the United States, one should always arrive exactly on time for dinner, a date, or a business appointment. While it is sometimes acceptable to arrive five minutes early, it is considered extremely impolite to arrive late. If other people are expected for dinner or for a meeting and you are late, everyone else will have to wait until you arrive to begin.

ANALYSIS

Decide whether you should arrive on time, early, or late in each of these situations. "On time" means at exactly the hour an event is scheduled to begin. Check your answers on page 165.

Situation	Early	On Time	Late
1. Job interview			
2. Take a test			
3. Attend class			
4. Go on a date			
5. Attend a dinner party			
6. Have a business appointment			
7. Catch a bus			
8. Attend a concert or a movie			
9. Meet a friend			
10. Attend church			
11. Go to a wedding			
12. Arrive at work			

LET'S SHARE

As you can see, most of the time, you are expected to arrive a little early or on time. However, in many cultures time is more flexible. Write five rules for time in your culture. Be sure to include specific situations and reasons.

1. _____

_____

2. _____

_____

3. _____

_____

4. _____

_____

5. _____

_____

When you have finished, share this information with the class.

NOW YOU DO IT

Complete these conversations.

1. JIM: I'd like you to have dinner with my family this Saturday night.
   YOU: _____
   JIM: That's great! Can you be at my house at 6:30 P.M.?
   YOU: _____
   JIM: I live at 420 Elm Street.
   YOU: _____
   JIM: Well, you go out Culver Road until you get to Main Street and
        then turn left. It's the second street on the right.
   YOU: _____
   JIM: Oh, you don't need to bring anything but yourself!
   YOU: Thanks for inviting me.
   JIM: _____
   YOU: See you at 6:30 P.M. on Saturday.
   JIM: _____

2. Sometimes you're unable to arrive on time even though you try to.
   Call your host, explain your reasons for being late, and give the time
   that you will arrive. (In this dialogue, you have gotten lost.)

   (Telephone rings.)
   JIM: Hello.
   YOU: _____
   JIM: Yes, we were wondering where you were. What happened?

95

You: _____

Jim: Where are you? Maybe I can give you directions to get here from where you are.

You: _____

Jim: Gee, you really *are* lost! The best thing to do is to drive back down Culver Road until you get to East High School and then turn left.

You: _____

Jim: Yes, that's about two miles. After you turn left at the high school, Elm Street will be the second street on your right. Understand? Repeat the directions back to me to make sure that you've got them.

You: _____

Jim: That's right. If you still can't find it, call me and I'll come get you. It's no trouble.

You: Thanks a lot. I'll be there by 7:30, I hope. I'm really sorry to be so much trouble.

Jim: _____

ROLE PLAY

Choose partners and role-play each of these situations. Be certain to use correct body language and facial expressions.

1. You and your friend have decided to attend a party, but neither of you is sure what time you should arrive. Ask the person giving the party about the correct time to come.

2. You plan to attend a very popular movie that has very long waiting lines. Decide with a friend whether you should attend the 7:30 P.M. or 9:45 P.M. show and what time you should arrive at the theater to get your tickets.

3. You wish to attend church services. Telephone the church office and ask the times of the services.

6 DINING OUT WITH FRIENDS

Some people, instead of inviting you to their home, will suggest going to a restaurant. Eating out is a difficult experience if you are unfamiliar with the foods or the idioms used to order them. Here are some helpful phrases and idioms used to place an order at a restaurant.

FORMAL SETTING

WAITER: Can I bring you something else, sir?

DINER: Yes, thank you. May we
see the dessert menu?

Formal setting

INFORMAL SETTING

WAITRESS: What'll it be?

DINER: I'd like a cheeseburger,
an order of fries, and a
chocolate shake.

Informal setting

As you can see, the language you use differs in each situation. In a less
formal environment, you may use contractions and speak in a more open,
friendly manner. In the following exercise, you will get practice responding
in both formal and informal situations.

NOW YOU DO IT

Complete each dialogue. Then role-play each with a partner. Be sure to use
correct gestures and body language.

97

1. You go to a coffee shop or ice cream parlor and order ice cream. The waiter brings you a glass of iced tea instead.

You: _____

WAITER: Yes. What can I do for you?

You: _____

WAITER: No. I'm certain you ordered iced tea.

You: _____

WAITER: I'm sorry. I'll bring you your ice cream. What flavor do you want?

You: _____

WAITER: Can I get you anything else?

You: _____

2. You are in a restaurant and see something on the menu that looks interesting, but you do not know what it is. Ask the waiter to explain the dish to you.

You: _____

WAITER: Yes, sir. How can I help you?

You: _____

WAITER: That is a beef patty cooked to your order and served on a seeded bun with our special sauce.

You: _____

WAITER: Well, the special sauce is made of mayonnaise, ketchup, pickles, and several spices.

You: _____

WAITER: I believe you would enjoy it. How would you like it cooked? Rare, medium, or well done?

You: _____

WAITER: Rare means the inside of the meat is very red, medium means the inside is pink, and well done means the meat is cooked completely.

You: _____

WAITER: Thank you. I'll bring your order shortly.

3. You are on a date with a friend at a restaurant. Decide what you wish to order from the menu and order it.

JIM: There seems to be a lot of delicious meals to choose from. What would you like?

You: _____

JIM: Well, I think I'll have the lasagna. They really make it well here.

YOU: _____

JIM: Their stuffed shells are good, too. You can get them stuffed with ricotta cheese or with meat.

YOU: _____

JIM: Order whatever you want. Perhaps if you get the stuffed shells, we could share.

YOU: _____

JIM: That sounds like a good idea.

YOU: _____

JIM: When the waitress comes back, I'll order our dinner. Would you like anything else?

YOU: _____

JIM: OK, it looks like we'll have a great dinner!

4. You are in the cafeteria or a fast-food restaurant. Order a sandwich of roast beef and lettuce on rye bread without mayonnaise.

SERVER: What'll you have?

YOU: _____

SERVER: What kind of bread?

YOU: _____

SERVER: Do you want anything on it?

YOU: _____

SERVER: Did you say you want lettuce and tomato?

YOU: _____

5. You are in a fast-food restaurant (McDonald's or Burger King). You have been waiting in line and now it is your turn. Order a hamburger with ketchup, no onions, french fries, and a large Coke.

SERVER: Can I help you?

YOU: _____

SERVER: To eat here or to go?

YOU: _____

SERVER: Do you want extra ketchup or salt? The packages are on that counter over there. Help yourself.

YOU: _____

SERVER: That'll be $2.45, please.

ROLE PLAY

Choose partners and role-play each of these situations.

1. You have been invited to a potluck dinner. Ask your hostess or host what you should bring, when the dinner starts, and what to wear.

2. A friend has offered to "fix you up with a blind date" for Saturday night. Ask your friend about this person and get him or her to suggest a place to take your blind date when you go out.

LEAVE-TAKING

The proper way to leave a party or social gathering is to say good-bye to the host and hostess and to thank them. Here are some examples of leave-taking.

Model Dialogues

1. GUEST: Thank you for a lovely evening.
   HOSTESS: I'm so glad you could come.
   GUEST: Good-bye.
   HOSTESS: Good-bye.

2. GUEST: Thank you for inviting me. I had a very good time.
   HOSTESS: So did we. Do come to visit us again soon.
   GUEST: I'd like that. Thanks again. Good-bye.
   HOSTESS: Good-bye.

3. GUEST: I have to go now. Thank you for the delicious meal.
   HOSTESS: You're very welcome. I'm glad you enjoyed it.
   GUEST: 'Bye.
   HOSTESS: Good-bye.

NOW YOU DO IT

After you have studied the examples of leave-taking, complete these dialogues. Then practice them with a partner, using correct gestures and body language. Remember to smile and shake hands as you leave.

1. You have attended a dinner party at your professor's house and are ready to leave.

YOU: _____

HOST: I'm so glad you enjoyed the dinner and meeting some new friends.

YOU: _____

HOST: Thank you. I hope you'll come to visit us again soon.

YOU: _____

HOST: Good-bye.

2. You have a 10:00 appointment. It is now 9:30 and you are sitting and talking with your friends. Tell them you have to leave.

YOU: _____

FRIEND: Why? It's only 9:30.

YOU: _____

FRIEND: Too bad. We're having such a good time!

YOU: _____

FRIEND: So long. See you in class.

YOU: _____

7 SIMULATION GAME: GOING TO A NIGHTCLUB*

In this section, you will have the opportunity to meet people, to dance, to order food and drinks, and to have a good time! Enjoy yourself! Try out the English you have learned in these situations to get points and to make new friends. Remember to ask questions if necessary and to use idioms as much as possible.

Setting Up the Game

To play this game, you will need the following:

1. *Personnel:* Waitress, waiter, hostess, bartender, entertainers (optional: taped music may be used for dancing)

   (Optional personnel: a drunk, a person who makes advances to the women participants)

2. *Equipment:* Waitress's order pads, checks, menu (can be handmade† from a local restaurant); paper money and change, credit cards, identification (can be handmade); table settings and refreshments (optional); "Please wait to be seated" sign, flowers and candles for tables, tablecloths; tables, chairs, and bar counter with chairs.

   Refreshments are optional; however, it adds atmosphere to provide "munchies" and soda for "patrons."

*For detailed directions, see the Appendix.
†A sample menu is given in the Appendix.

101

3. *Setup:* In one section of the room, place tables (some with four chairs, others with two) in restaurant style. If possible, decorate them with tablecloths, candles, and flowers to create a realistic setting. In another part of the room, set up a "bar" with several chairs or stools. You can use a long table for this. Be certain to leave enough space beside the bar and tables for a dance floor.

4. Read the directions in the Appendix.

POINT ACTIVITIES

1. Go over to someone you do not know, introduce yourself, and shake hands.

   Point value: 2   Signature _____

2. After you introduce yourself to someone, carry on a conversation for three minutes.

   Point value: 3   Signature _____

3. Ask if you can buy someone a drink, or accept a drink from another person.

   Point value: 3   Signature _____

4. Order a drink of your choice at the bar and pay for it.

   Point value: 2   Signature _____

5. Ask someone to dance and then dance for one full dance.

   Point value: 5   Signature _____

6. The bartender brings you the wrong drink. Ask him to give you the correct drink.

   Point value: 4   Signature _____

7. Invite someone to a party you are giving next Saturday night.

   Point value: 3   Signature _____

8. You see someone you would really like to meet. Find a way to meet this person.

   Point value: 2   Signature _____

9. Introduce a friend of yours to someone you have just met.

   Point value: 2   Signature _____

10. Ask someone you have met and talked with during this exercise to go out with you in the future. This may be someone of the same sex or

of the opposite sex. Make specific plans including time, date, activity, and place of meeting.

Point value: *same sex*, 3   Signature _____

opposite sex, 8   Signature _____

11. There is a drunk at the bar who is annoying you. Handle this situation.

Point value: 4   Signature _____

12. A person of the opposite sex whom you do not know is annoying you by making improper advances. Handle the situation.

Point value: 10   Signature _____

13. You are at the restaurant with a friend of the opposite sex. Converse with your date and order a meal from the menu.

Point value: 3   Signature _____

14. You wish to know where the rest room is. Ask where it is located.

Point value: 3   Signature _____

15. You wish to order more food or a dessert. Get the attention of the waiter or waitress and order.

Point value: 2   Signature _____

16. You see something on the menu that looks interesting but you do not know what it is. Ask the waiter to explain the dish to you.

Point value: 2   Signature _____

17. You wish to order wine with your dinner. Ask to see a wine list and order the wine of your choice.

Point value: 2   Signature _____

18. When your dinner is brought to you, it is not hot or doesn't taste right. Get the waiter's attention and send the food back to the kitchen.

Point value: 5   Signature _____

19. You have had dinner and wish to pay your bill. Get the waiter's attention and ask for your check.

Point value: 2   Signature _____

20. When you receive your check, you notice that an item that you did not order or receive has been included in the charge. Ask for your check to be corrected.

Point value: 6   Signature _____

21. You pay for your check and receive incorrect change. Ask for the correct change.

Point value: 5   Signature _____

seven

Shopping in the United States

hich of these items would you expect to find in a large American grocery store?

Fresh vegetables	Flowers and gardening supplies
Meats	Cards and wrapping paper
Magazines	Paper products
Baked goods	Medicines
Clothing	Toys
Fabric	Dishes and silverware
Soap and waxes	Small appliances
Dog and cat food	Rat poison and bug killers
Diapers	Small tools
Batteries	Books
Imported foods	Frozen foods
Fast foods	Salad bars
Cereals	Potted plants

You would probably find all of these items!

1 PLACES TO SHOP

Shopping in the United States is exciting and challenging. The consumer is offered an almost limitless selection of merchandise in all price ranges and sizes. Through shopping, you can sharpen your English skills as you ask questions, select products, and sometimes even bargain for the best price at garage sales and farm markets.

MATCHING

At one time in the United States, people shopped in a different store for each type of product. They went to a bakery for bread, to a butcher shop for meat, and to a pharmacy for medicine. Today, specialized stores still exist, but people may also shop in one store for many items.

In the column on the left is a list of stores. In the column on the right are items you can purchase in these stores. Match the store with the items it sells. The answers are on page 165.

_____ 1. Furniture store	A.	Bread, rolls, cakes, doughnuts, bagels, cookies
_____ 2. Department store	B.	Necklaces, rings, earrings, watches, bracelets
_____ 3. Automotive supplier	C.	Small animals, animal supplies
_____ 4. Florist	D.	Parts to fix cars and trucks
_____ 5. Jeweler	E.	Tables, chairs, lamps, beds, sofas, bookcases
_____ 6. Pet store	F.	Clothing, appliances, linen, paper goods, jewelery, perfume
_____ 7. Appliance store	G.	Tools, supplies for maintaining the home
_____ 8. Drugstore	H.	Refrigerators, washing machines, stoves, dryers, dishwashers
_____ 9. Hardware store	I.	Records, tapes, and machines for playing them
_____ 10. Nursery	J.	Trees, plants, gardening supplies
_____ 11. Record store	K.	Flower arrangements, corsages, potted plants
_____ 12. Bakery	L.	Medicines, often other items like candy, school supplies, magazines, and shampoo

OTHER SHOPPING OPTIONS

Besides regular retail stores, there are other places to shop where items are often less expensive.

Lawn sale Garage sale Porch sale Yard sale Household sale	People sell used merchandise at their home. They set up the sale in the yard, garage, or driveway, or on the porch.
Farmer's market	Farmers bring their farm produce to one location to sell. Foods are usually fresher and less expensive than in a store.

| Flea market | People sell antiques, used merchandise, and new items at discounted prices. |

These sales are often listed in the want-ads section of the newspaper. At such sales, you may bargain for a lower price.

MODEL DIALOGUES

Talking to salespeople at a *department store*.

1. YOU: Excuse me, can you tell me where the dresses are?
   SALESPERSON: Do you want children's, juniors', or misses' dresses?
   YOU: I don't know the difference.
   SALESPERSON: Children's has clothes for infants and children through age 10 or 11. Juniors' are for teens and women who are small. Misses are for regular-size women.
   YOU: I see. Where are the juniors' dresses located?*

2. SALESPERSON: Can I help you?
   YOU: No, thank you. I'm just looking.

3. SALESPERSON: Can I help you?
   YOU: Yes, I'd like to pay for this. Can you tell me how much the sales tax on this item is?
   SALESPERSON: The sales tax is seven percent.
   YOU: Thank you.
   SALESPERSON: Do you know you can't return bathing suits or underwear for sanitary reasons?
   YOU: Thanks for telling me. May I have a box instead of a bag for the bathing suit?
   SALESPERSON: Certainly. Is this purchase cash, check, or credit card?
   YOU: Cash.

Talking to the seller at a *garage sale*.

4. SELLER: Hi. How are you?
   YOU: Fine, thanks.
   SELLER: Are you interested in anything in particular?
   YOU: Yes, does this can opener work?
   SELLER: I think so. Let's plug it in and see.
   YOU: How much is it?
   SELLER: Five dollars.
   YOU: That's a lot of money for a used can opener. Can you give me a better price?
   SELLER: Well, I can let you have it for three in cash.
   YOU: OK. That sounds like a good deal.
   SELLER: All sales are final, you know. I'm sorry I don't have any bags to put it into.
   YOU: That's OK. Thanks.

*See size chart on page 166.

Reread the model dialogues and see how many differences you can find between shopping at a regular store and shopping at a garage sale or flea market.

LET'S SHARE

List some things about shopping that are different in your country. Share them with your class when you are finished.

1. _____

_____

2. _____

_____

3. _____

_____

2 TALKING WITH SALESPEOPLE

QUICK CUSTOMS QUIZ

Below are situations in which you might find yourself in the United States. Read each situation, decide what is appropriate, and choose the answer that best fits the circumstance. Draw a circle around the letter in front of your answer. Check your answers against those on page 165, which are the answers an American would probably give.

1. You are in a department store because you wish to look but have no intention of buying anything. A salesperson comes up to you and asks, "May I help you?" What should you do?

   a. Say no.
   b. Say yes and ask for help so you won't offend the salesperson.
   c. Say, "Thanks, but I'm just browsing."

2. When reading a newspaper or magazine, you notice something called a manufacturer's coupon that offers to give you 10 to 15 cents off the price of a particular product. Since you wish to save money, what should you do?

   a. Take the whole newspaper to the store and give it to the clerk when you pay for your groceries.

b. When you are paying for your groceries, tell the clerk that you saw the coupons in the paper and want the discount.

c. Neatly cut out the coupon and take it with you to the store. Give it to the clerk when you pay for the product.

3. You see a suit that you really like but think the price is too high. What should you do?

a. If you can afford it for the price, buy it.
b. Offer the clerk less money for it.
c. Tell the clerk that the suit is not worth that much money.
d. Look for the same suit at another store where it may cost less.

4. You wish to purchase some new clothes in the United States but are not sure of what size you wear in American sizes. What should you do?

a. Ask the salesperson for help.
b. Try on clothes until you find the size that fits you.
c. Ask friends who have been living in America longer what size you should wear.

5. You find a garment that you really like but are not sure that it will fit you. What should you do?

a. Buy it. You can always return it if it doesn't fit.
b. Put it on over your clothes.
c. Measure it against your body.
d. Take it to the rest room and try it on.
e. Ask to try on the garment in a fitting room.

6. You wish to buy a used car and have just found the one you want on a used-car lot. The salesman offers you a 30-day warranty and will reduce the price by $100. What should you do?

a. Ask a mechanic who does not work at the used car lot to check the car to make sure that it's in good condition.
b. Go to other used-car lots to compare prices on similar cars.
c. Buy the car before someone else does.
d. Ask the salesman to lower the price by another $50.
e. Ask to have the warranty in writing and make sure you understand what it covers.

IDIOMS AND PHRASES

Here are some phrases you will find helpful when you need to ask for information. The italicized words are key phrases that can be adapted both to ask questions and to answer them.

1. YOU: *Can you recommend* a gift I can send my sister?
SALESPERSON: Perhaps she'd like some perfume.

2. YOU: *What* other colors do these shirts come in?
SALESPERSON: They come in red, blue, and white.

3. You: *Can you tell me* what size I need to buy?
   SALESPERSON: I think a medium would fit you well.

4. You: *How do I* return this if it does not match the color of my living room?
   SALESPERSON: Bring your receipt and we'll refund your money or exchange it for one in another color.

5. You: *Where can I find* the corn flakes?
   SALESPERSON: They're in aisle two.

NOW YOU DO IT

Complete these practice dialogues. Then role-play them with a partner, using correct gestures and body language.

1. Ask the druggist to recommend an effective dandruff shampoo.

DRUGGIST: Hello. Can I help you?

You: _____

DRUGGIST: There are several brands available. What are your symptoms?

You: _____

DRUGGIST: I see. Well, you could try Ridruff or Hair and Scalp.

You: _____

DRUGGIST: Ridruff is medicated and is about a dollar more expensive than Hair and Scalp. But either shampoo will do the job, I think.

You: _____

DRUGGIST: The shampoos are located on the third shelf, beside the hair sprays.

You: _____

2. You want to buy some perfume as a gift for your friend Ann's birthday. Ask a mutual friend what kind of perfume she uses because you like the way her perfume smells.

You: _____

FRIEND: Fine. How's it going?

You: _____

FRIEND: That is a problem. Sometimes I have trouble getting presents for my friends, too.

You: _____

FRIEND: Thanks a lot. It's nice of you to notice. My perfume is called Wintersong.

You: _____

FRIEND: Yes, I think Ann will like it.

YOU: _____

FRIEND: OK. See you later.

3. You have an advertisement from the paper, and you wish to have a salesperson help you find the merchandise.

YOU: _____

SALESPERSON: Yes, they're over here.

YOU: I can't find my size. Do you have any more?

SALESPERSON: No, we . . .

YOU: I want the sweater you have advertised, not a higher-priced one.

SALESPERSON: Well, I can give you a "rain check."

YOU: _____

SALESPERSON: Yes, you can buy the sweater at the same price when we get it in stock.

YOU: _____

SALESPERSON: Probably later in the week.

YOU: _____

3 PROBLEMS AND SOLUTIONS

Sometimes, even though you have shopped carefully, you must return an item to the store or have it repaired by the store. Here are some informative situations that will help you deal with these problems.

QUICK CUSTOMS QUIZ

Below are situations in which you might find yourself in the United States. Read each situation, decide what is appropriate, and choose the answer that best fits the circumstance. Draw a circle around the letter in front of your answer. Check your answers against those on page 166, which are the answers an American would probably give.

1. You wish to return something you bought a month ago. You've never used it but haven't had the opportunity to bring it back. At the store, the clerk tells you that since you bought the item more than seven days ago, you cannot return it. What should you do?

a. Show the clerk that the tickets are still on the item and that you haven't used it.
b. Ask to see the manager.
c. Tell the clerk you'll never shop in the store again.
d. Explain that you didn't know that merchandise had to be returned within seven days.
e. Thank the clerk and leave.

2. You received a shirt as a gift for your birthday. You like the shirt but find it is too small. What should you do?

a. Nothing. Keep it because it is a gift.
b. Go to the store where your friend bought the shirt and exchange it for a larger size.
c. Tell your friend to get you a larger size.
d. Give it to someone else as a gift.

3. You've bought a refrigerator and it breaks down during the first 30 days you own it. A friend tells you not to worry because the refrigerator is under warranty. What does this mean?

a. The store where you bought it will fix the refrigerator free if you call and tell them about it.
b. If the refrigerator is broken through normal use, the manufacturer will fix it free of charge.
c. You should call a service company and have the machine fixed.

4. You have been receiving in the mail magazines that you did not order. What should you do?

a. Write to the company and tell them there has been a mistake.
b. Send the magazines back.
c. Keep the magazines and do nothing.
d. Pay for the magazines when the bill comes.

5. You open a jar of applesauce and inside it you find a few pieces of broken glass. Fortunately, you have not eaten any of the applesauce. What should you do?

a. Throw it away.
b. Take out the glass and eat the rest.
c. Return the applesauce and the jar to the store where you bought it and tell them about the broken glass.

ANALYSIS

1. In the United States, "the customer is always right." This means that most businesses try to please the customer and will go out of their way to provide the product and services the customer wants. Is this true in your country? Why? Discuss an example with your class.

2. How is business different in your country from business in the United States? For example, do items have warranties that allow purchasers to return them if they don't work? Will stores fix or replace products if they break down during the warranty period, or is the customer responsible if an item breaks down? Can customers return merchandise to stores or exchange it for other goods?

3. How do American stores differ from stores in your country? Can you pay by check or credit card? Are there only specialized stores, or are there also department stores that sell many types of merchandise?

NOW YOU DO IT

Complete these conversations. Then practice them aloud with a partner. Be sure to use appropriate gestures and body language. Speak with expression!

1. You wish to return a coat that you purchased by check from a department store.

You: I'd like to return this coat, please.

Salesperson: What's wrong with it?

You: _____

Salesperson: OK, do you have your receipt?

You: _____

Salesperson: Do you want to exchange it for another coat, or do you want your money back?

You: _____

Salesperson: I'm really sorry you had problems with the coat.

You: _____

2. You have purchased an expensive watch, and after 30 days, it stops working. You have your receipt and want the store to repair or replace it.

Salesperson: Can I help you?

You: _____

Salesperson: Do you have your receipt?

You: _____

Salesperson: OK, but we can't fix it here. We'll have to send it to Chicago to be repaired.

You: _____

Salesperson: It could take as long as three or four months. Is that OK? Service is really slow with this watch manufacturer.

You: _____

SALESPERSON: Well, I'm not sure we can replace it after 30 days. I'll have to ask the manager.

YOU: _____

SALESPERSON: He says we can replace it but we don't have this watch in stock now. What do you want me to do?

YOU: _____

SALESPERSON: Yes, we can order you one from our Northside store. That will only take one day. I'm really sorry that you have had to go through all the trouble and that I can't help you today.

YOU: _____

3. You wish to buy a sweater in a department store.

SALESPERSON: May I help you?

YOU: _____

SALESPERSON: They're located over here. What size do you need?

YOU: _____

SALESPERSON: Are you looking for a particular color to match something?

YOU: Yes. _____

SALESPERSON: This one looks like what you've described.

YOU: No, I'd rather have _____

SALESPERSON: How about this one? Would you like to try it on?

YOU: _____

SALESPERSON: The fitting rooms are located in the back of this department. I'll take you.

YOU: _____

SALESPERSON: Let me know if I can help you.

YOU: _____

ROLE PLAY

Now that we've covered shopping through conversation, let's put your knowledge into practice. Choose a partner and role-play each of these situations. Discuss the situation first, decide on appropriate dialogue, and practice using appropriate body language and gestures. Then take turns with other class members acting out these situations.

1. You wish to buy your friend a birthday present but do not know his or her size. Ask a salesperson to help you select a shirt for your friend. Be

sure to describe your friend carefully and tell the salesperson the type and color of shirt you are looking for.

2. You are in a hardware store and pay cash for a tool. When you count your change, you find that your change is 87 cents less than it should be. Get the sales clerk to give you the correct change.

3. You get your purchase home from the store and discover that it is damaged. Take it back to the store and get your money back. Be sure to have your receipt with you!

4 SIMULATION GAME: SHOPPING IN THE UNITED STATES*

Here is a chance to go shopping! Choose as many activities as you wish and try to complete them within the time limits set by your instructor. As you complete each exercise, be sure to get the signature of the person you speak or work with.

Setting Up the Game

To play this game, you will need the following:

1. *Personnel:* Cashier, two or more clerks (depending on class size)
2. *Equipment:* Play money and play change for players and cashier; play credit cards, identification, checks for players; receipt pad, sales slips for salespeople; good selection of men's and women's clothing (ask students to bring items to class for use in the game); tables for clothing; partition to mark off fitting room (students will not actually try on clothes); desk area for clerk
3. *Special considerations:* Carefully display and tag merchandise before the game. Train facilitators for their roles and encourage them to be helpful and polite, although at times, they may choose to be pushy. Ask the cashier to be strict about returns and to request proper information to cash checks or to OK credit cards. Do not allow students to take merchandise from the "store" because it will be needed for the rest of the players. Have salespeople keep merchandise orderly during the game.
4. *Setup:* In the center of the room, arrange merchandise on three tables: one for women's clothing, one for men's clothing, and one for assorted merchandise. Designate one corner of the room as the fitting room (students will not actually try on clothing). Place the cashier at a desk near the door so that players will have to pass it to leave the room. Make certain you have all the cashier's props (money, receipts, etc.) at the cashier's table. You may label the areas with signs.

*For detailed directions, see the Appendix.

POINT ACTIVITIES

1. You wish to buy a blouse, shirt, or sweater. Ask the clerk to help you find your size. Tell the clerk your size and the kind of garment you would like (length, color, fabric, purpose, etc.).

    Point value: 3   Signature _____

2. You wish to look at merchandise but have no intention of buying. The clerk approaches you and offers to help you. Handle the situation.

    Point value: 2   Signature _____

3. You wish to buy new clothes but know that the weather is very different here than in your native country. Ask the salesperson what he or she would recommend.

    Point value: 3   Signature _____

4. You find a garment you like but are not sure it will fit you. Ask to try on the garment in the fitting room.

    Point value: 2   Signature _____

5. You have found a garment that you wish to buy. You wish to pay for it with a personal check or credit card. Take the garment to the cashier and pay for it.

    Point value: 3   Signature _____

6. You wish to purchase a garment for a friend, but you are not certain of his or her size. Ask the clerk for help (describe your friend and answer the clerk's questions).

    Point value: 4   Signature _____

7. You have purchased a garment, and when you get home, you find that it is stained or torn. Return the garment to the store and get your money back.

    Point value: 5   Signature _____

8. You have received from a friend a gift that he says he purchased in this store. You wish to exchange it for another color or size. Convince the clerk to let you make the exchange.

    Point value: 5   Signature _____

9. You wish to exchange a gift that a friend has gotten you from this store for another size or color. However, when you ask to return the garment, the clerk tells you that the store will not accept returns without a receipt and that there is no proof that your friend bought the garment at this store. Handle the situation tactfully, but try to convince the clerk to let you make the exchange.

    Point value: 5   Signature _____

10. You have paid for a garment in cash. When you count your change, you find that you are short 57 cents. Get the cashier to give you the correct change.

    Point value: 4   Signature _____

11. You would like to buy a garment, but you see that sizes are different in the United States than they are in your country. Ask a salesperson or a fellow shopper to help you find your size.

    Point value: 2   Signature _____

12. You have chosen two garments but cannot decide which you like better. Ask your friends to help you decide which one to buy.

    Point value: 1   Signature _____

13. Both you and another shopper wish to purchase the same item of clothing. Convince the other person to let you buy the article.

    Point value: 5   Signature _____

eight

Using the Telephone

n American visiting another English-speaking country was expecting few differences when using the telephone. From the airport, she called her friend to pick her up. Although she carefully inserted the correct coins, all she could hear was the person at the other end of the line saying, "Hello, hello, hello!" She tried to explain where she was and what she wanted, but the other person couldn't hear her. Finally, her friend realized what was happening and told her, "If you want to talk, you have to push the button on the phone!"

Have you ever had an experience like this with a telephone? If so, share it with your class.

In this chapter, we'll discuss how to use the telephone for business and social occasions.

1 LEARNING ABOUT THE TELEPHONE

MATCHING

There are many terms you will need to know to use the telephone in the United States. Match the terms in the left column with their meaning in the right column. Check your answers on page 167.

_____ 1. Person-to-person call

_____ 2. Wrong number

A. Broken; not working

B. The three-digit number preceding a telephone number that indicates the city and area in which it is located.

_____ 3. Toll-free number

C. The person who receives the long-distance call must pay for the call

_____ 4. Area code

D. A long-distance call that the caller dials without help from the operator

_____ 5. Operator

E. A number that is not the number you wished to reach

_____ 6. Unlisted number

F. A telephone number that is neither listed in the telephone book nor available from the operator

_____ 7. Receiver

G. An employee of the telephone company who assists people in making calls

_____ 8. Party line

H. A telephone call made within your calling area; there is no charge for this

_____ 9. Long-distance call

I. The part of the telephone that you hold against your ear to speak and listen.

_____ 10. Local call

J. A call made outside your calling area. These calls usually cost more and require dialing 0 or 1 plus the number of the person with whom you wish to speak.

_____ 11. Out of order

K. A telephone connection that is shared by two or more customers; this costs less than a private line, which is used by only one customer

_____ 12. Busy signal

L. A long-distance call that is free of charge to the caller; many large businesses and hotels provide such a number, which usually begins with 1-800

_____ 13. Station-to-station _or_ direct-distance call

M. A call made with operator assistance to a particular person

_____ 14. Collect call

N. A beeping noise that indicates that someone is talking on the phone

MODEL DIALOGUES

Talking with the operator:

1. OPERATOR: Hello. This is the operator. Can I help you?
   JEFF: Yes, I'd like to make a person-to-person collect call to Peter Strong at (617) 872-9012. My name is Jeff Bridges.
   OPERATOR: Just a moment. (*makes call*) I have a collect person-to-person call for Peter Strong from Jeff Bridges. Will you accept the charges?
   PETER: Yes, this is Peter Strong. I'll accept the charges.
   OPERATOR: Go ahead, please.

2. OPERATOR: This is the operator. What city, please?
   YOU: Boca Raton, Florida.
   OPERATOR: Yes, go ahead, please.
   YOU: I'd like the phone number of George Snell at 369 Glade Road.
   OPERATOR: I'm sorry, that number is unlisted.
   YOU: Thank you.

TALKING WITH THE OPERATOR

1. Call information for the telephone number of Brette Simms at 1764 Walton Avenue, The Bronx, New York City.

OPERATOR: Operator.

YOU: _____

OPERATOR: You've reached the local operator. Please call area code (212) 555-1212 to get that information. An information operator will give you the number.

YOU: _____

INFORMATION OPERATOR: What city?

YOU: _____

INFORMATION OPERATOR: OK. Can I help you?

YOU: I'd like the number for Brett Simms, please.

INFORMATION OPERATOR: How do you spell that name?

YOU: B-R-E-T-T S-I-M-M-S

INFORMATION OPERATOR: Is that *b* as in *boy*, *r* as in *Robert*, *e* as in *exit*, *t* as in *Thomas*, *t* as in *Thomas*, *e* as in *exit*, and *s* as in *Susan*, *i* as in *Indian*, *m* as in *money*, *m* as in *money*, and *s* as in *Susan*?

YOU: _____

INFORMATION OPERATOR: Do you have an address for the party?

YOU: _____

INFORMATION OPERATOR: That party can be reached at 299-8063.

YOU: _____

2. You wish to reverse the charges on a long-distance call. This means that the operator will ask the person you are calling if he or she will pay for the call. Dial 0 plus the ten digits of number you wish to reach.

OPERATOR: Can I help you?

YOU: _____

OPERATOR: What is your name, please?

YOU: _____

OPERATOR: One minute, please. (*phone rings*)

PERSON: Hello.

OPERATOR: This is the operator. I have a collect call from _____. Will you accept the charges?

PARTY: _____

OPERATOR: Go ahead.

3. You are away from home and wish to charge a long-distance call to your home phone. Dial 0 plus the ten digits of the number you wish to reach.

OPERATOR: This is the operator. Can I help you?

YOU: _____

OPERATOR: What's your home phone number?

YOU: _____

OPERATOR: What is your name and address?

YOU: _____

OPERATOR: Please spell your name.

YOU: _____

OPERATOR: Is anyone at that number now?

YOU: _____

OPERATOR: I'll connect your call. Please hold.

YOU: _____

2 TALKING ON THE TELEPHONE

Sometimes we have problems with the telephone. We get the wrong number, someone calls us by mistake, or someone has trouble understanding what the other person is saying. All these situations require telephone courtesy and understanding. Practice these model conversations with a partner.

MODEL DIALOGUES

1. You accidentally dial the wrong number.

PERSON: Hello.

YOU: May I speak with Dr. McGuire?

PERSON: You have the wrong number.

YOU: I do?

PERSON: What number did you dial?

YOU: 239-8063.

PERSON: This is 8064. Try it again.

YOU: I'm sorry to have bothered you.

PERSON: That's OK. Good-bye.

2. Someone dials your number by mistake.

YOU: Hello.

PERSON: Is Terry there?

YOU: There is no one here by that name.

PERSON: Are you sure?

YOU: Yes, I'm sure. You have the wrong number.

PERSON: Is this 645-9234?

YOU: No, it isn't.

PERSON: I'm terribly sorry.

YOU: That's OK. Good-bye.

3. You have just dialed the wrong number. It was a long-distance call, and you don't want to be charged for your mistake.

OPERATOR: This is the operator. May I help you?

YOU: Yes, I dialed (716) 433-6947 and got the wrong number.

OPERATOR: I'm sorry. Do you know what number you reached?

YOU: No, I don't.

OPERATOR: What is your number?

YOU: (212) 789-4982.

OPERATOR: I'll credit your account and place the call for you.

YOU: Thank you.

QUICK CUSTOMS QUIZ

Below are situations in which you might find yourself in the United States. Read each situation, decide what is appropriate, and choose the answer that best fits the circumstance. Draw a circle around the letter in front of your answer. Check your answers against those on page 167, which are the answers an American would probably give. Then discuss with your classmates how you would handle these situations in your country.

1. The telephone company sent you a bill, which you paid. Now you have received a letter that states that you never paid the bill. What should you do?

   a. Nothing. You know you've paid.
   b. Find proof that you've paid them (canceled check or receipt), copy it, and send it to the telephone company.
   c. Call them and explain the situation.

2. When you answer the telephone, the caller asks for someone who does not live there. Obviously the caller has the wrong number. What should you do?

   a. Hang up.
   b. Begin a conversation.
   c. Tell the caller he or she has reached the wrong number.
   d. Tell the caller your number and ask what number he or she dialed.

3. You have made a long-distance call, which you've dialed directly. Unfortunately, you dialed the wrong number and were connected with someone in another state. What should you do?

   a. Nothing.
   b. Call the operator and tell her about your mistake.
   c. Refuse to pay for the call when you get your bill.
   d. Dial again and hope you get the party you wanted.
   e. Check the phone number and make sure you have written it down correctly.

4. You have called a place of business. The receptionist answers, "Stephans Air Conditioning. Please hold." Then you hear a click and silence. What should you do?

   a. Hang up.
   b. Yell into the phone, "Hello, hello, is anyone there?"
   c. Keep the phone to your ear and wait.
   d. Hang up and call back.

5. You are talking on the phone with someone, and all of a sudden there is silence. The other person is not there any longer. What should you do?

    a. Hang up. He or she obviously didn't want to talk with you any more and hung up.

    b. Hang up and call back. Obviously something went wrong with the telephone.

    c. Hang on until the connection is restored.

6. Someone calls your house, says obscene words, and tries to talk to you. What should you do?

    a. Hang up.

    b. Yell at the person.

    c. Talk to the person.

    d. Ask the person's name.

    e. Tell the person your name.

    f. Call the phone company and complain.

7. You have called an airline, and someone has said, "Hello, Flight Time Airline. No one is available now to take your call. Please stay on the line until the next available attendant can handle your call." You hear a click, and music begins to play. What should you do?

    a. Hang up.

    b. Hold the line and wait.

    c. Call the airline back later.

    d. Call the operator because there is trouble with the phone.

8. You have called a plumber to fix a leaky faucet. When you call, you hear the following taped message; "Hello, this is Joe the Plumber. I'm not here now. At the sound of the tone, please leave your name, phone number, and the nature of the problem. I'll contact you as soon as I can." Then you hear a beep. What should you do?

    a. Hang up.

    b. Hold the line and wait.

    c. State your name, phone number, and the problem you're having. Then hang up.

    d. Ask for him to repeat that.

    e. Tell him that you don't speak English very well and that he should speak more slowly.

9. You call the operator from a friend's house and ask to have the call you are about to make charged to your home phone number. What do you expect her to do?

    a. Bill the person you are calling for the call.

    b. Bill you at your home phone number for the cost of the call.

    c. Bill the call to the number from which you are calling.

10. When you answer the phone, you hear, "Hello, this is the operator. I have a collect call for anyone from Ralph Cummings. Will you accept the charges?" What should you do?

   a. Say yes if you wish to pay for the call from Ralph Cummings.
   b. Say no if you do not wish to pay for the call or if you do not know the person making the call.
   c. Ask the operator why she has called.

11. You make a phone call. When the ringing stops you hear, "The number you have dialed has been temporarily disconnected. This is a recording." What should you do?

   a. Ask the person to repeat that.
   b. Say, "What? I don't understand."
   c. Hang up, check the number in the phone book, and dial again.

12. You have called an operator for assistance in making a long-distance call. The operator tells you, "You can dial that direct." What should you do?

   a. Hang up and dial the number yourself.
   b. Ask the operator to help you.
   c. Hang up and call the operator back.

LET'S SHARE

1. Share with your classmates an interesting experience you have had using the telephone in your country and in the United States.
2. What is different about using or owning telephones in your country? Share this information with your class.

3 BUSINESS AND SOCIAL USES OF THE TELEPHONE

Telephones play an interesting role in life in the United States. In addition to being used for business purposes and to relay information, they are used to socialize. Americans who find themselves separated by distance from family and friends call to keep in touch. They telephone family members on birthdays and holidays if they cannot visit. In most families, the members who use the telephone the most are teenagers who call friends after school. Sometimes parents buy a second phone for their children to use.

LET'S SHARE

1. Who uses the phone most in your family?
2. Do people have several telephones in their homes in your country?

A secretary using the phone for business   A teenager using the phone

3. Are telephones used instead of visiting someone?
4. Look at the above photos of Americans using the telephone. Do these photos reflect how people in your country use the telephone?

IDIOMS AND PHRASES

Let's consider some phrases that are commonly used on the telephone. Study them carefully and use them in the conversation sections as well as when you use the telephone.

1. RECEPTIONIST: Will you hold?
   CALLER: Yes.

2. RECEPTIONIST: (*formal*) May I tell Dr. Smith who is calling?
   CALLER: Certainly. This is Jim Jones.

3. RECEPTIONIST: (*informal*) Who's calling? Who is this?
   CALLER: Jim Jones.

4. OTHER PERSON: Whom do you want to speak to? *or* To whom do you wish to speak?
   CALLER: I would like to speak to Aimee Cummings.
   OTHER PERSON: She isn't here right now. Can I take a message?
   CALLER: (*formal*) Yes, please ask her to return my call at 654-9234 *or* (*informal*) Please have her call me back at 654-9234.

MODEL DIALOGUES

1. OTHER PERSON: You have the wrong number.
   CALLER: I'm sorry. (*hangs up*)

2. CALLER: Hello, may I speak with José Gomez?
   OTHER PERSON: I'm sorry. You have the wrong number.
   CALLER: Is this 234-9874?
   OTHER PERSON: No. I'm sorry. Good-bye.

3. OTHER PERSON: Hello. This is Joe's Pizza. Can I help you?
   CALLER: Yes. I'd like a large cheese and sausage pizza.
   OTHER PERSON: Do you want anything else?
   CALLER: Yes, I'd like four mixed salads and four Cokes.
   OTHER PERSON: What is your address?
   CALLER: I live at 435 Melville Street.
   OTHER PERSON: That comes to ten thirty-four. We'll deliver your order
   in about twenty-five minutes.
   CALLER: Thanks. I'll be looking for you.

4. CALLER: Hello. This is Anna Joseph. May I please speak with Elise
   Eisenburg?
   OTHER PERSON: I'm sorry, but she's not here now. Can I take a message?
   CALLER: Yes. Please tell her I called to ask her about the math homework. Ask her to call me this evening at 654-9234.
   OTHER PERSON: OK. I'll tell her as soon as she gets home.
   CALLER: Thank you. Good-bye.
   OTHER PERSON: 'Bye.

NOW YOU DO IT

Complete these conversations using the phrases and idioms you have learned.

Talking with friends:

1. Call a friend to say you'll be late.

FRIEND: Hello.

YOU: _____

FRIEND: Who is this?

YOU: _____

FRIEND: What's the matter?

YOU: _____

FRIEND: OK. See you soon.

YOU: _____

2. Someone calls to speak with your sister. She is not home. Take a message.

YOU: Hello.

CALLER: Can I speak with Aimee?

YOU: _____

CALLER: Oh, when do you expect her?

YOU: _____

CALLER: Can you give her a message?

YOU: _____

CALLER: Please tell her that Jennifer Schaefer called and ask her to call me back at 654-9234.

YOU: _____

CALLER: Good-bye. And thanks a lot.

YOU: _____

3. You call to talk with Brette. She is not home. Leave a message for her to call you back and give the time and phone number.

OTHER PERSON: Hello.

YOU: _____

OTHER PERSON: She's not home now.

YOU: _____

OTHER PERSON: She won't be in until after seven o'clock. Who is calling, please?

YOU: _____

OTHER PERSON: Can I take a message?

YOU: _____

OTHER PERSON: OK. I'll be glad to tell her that.

YOU: _____

OTHER PERSON: Good-bye.

4. A friend whom you haven't seen for a while calls you.

YOU: Hello.

PETE: Hello. This is Pete Howser. How are you?

YOU: _____

PETE: I haven't talked with you in a long time, so I thought I'd call to see how things are going.

YOU: _____

PETE: Well, what's new?

YOU: _____

PETE: I got a part-time job working at Ackley's, in the shoe department.

You: _____

PETE: The pay's not great, but it's a good place to get on-the-job experience. We even get a ten percent discount on merchandise. That'll come in handy at Christmas.

You: _____

PETE: Listen. I'm having some friends over Saturday night. Can you come?

You: _____

PETE: That's great. See you then.

You: _____

Using the phone for business:

1. Call for a dentist appointment.

RECEPTIONIST: Hello. Dr. Andrews's office.

You: _____

RECEPTIONIST: Who's calling, please?

You: _____

RECEPTIONIST: Are you one of Dr. Andrews's patients?

You: _____

RECEPTIONIST: Is this an appointment for a checkup, or are you in pain?

You: _____

RECEPTIONIST: Can you come in next Monday at ten-thirty in the morning?

You: _____

RECEPTIONIST: I see. Would you prefer an evening appointment?

You: _____

RECEPTIONIST: The doctor had a cancellation and can see you this Thursday evening at seven-thirty.

You: _____

RECEPTIONIST: You're welcome. See you then.

2. Call a taxi to pick you up at 6:00 tomorrow morning to take you to the airport.

RECEPTIONIST: Prompt Cab Company.

You: _____

RECEPTIONIST: What's the name, please?

You: _____

RECEPTIONIST: Where do you want us to pick you up?

YOU: _____

RECEPTIONIST: When do you want us to pick you up?

YOU: _____

RECEPTIONIST: Where are you going?

YOU: _____

RECEPTIONIST: OK. Wait out front. The cabbie will be by at six.

YOU: _____

RECEPTIONIST: About seven dollars.

YOU: _____

RECEPTIONIST: Thank you for calling Prompt Cab. Good-bye.

LET'S SHARE

1. From what you have learned so far, how is using the telephone different in your country? List five differences.
2. Do people in your country use the telephone to visit with a relative or friend?
3. What do you say when you answer the telephone in your country?
4. Most people in the United States have a telephone. Is this true in your country? If not, how do people communicate with people in their town or with those who live far away?
5. In the United States, teenagers have the reputation for staying on the telephone for a long time. In fact, some American families have two phone numbers, one for the parents and one for the children. Is this true in your country? Do teenagers use the telephone to visit with their friends? Discuss how you feel about this.

4 USING THE DIRECTORY

The telephone directory, or phone book, is an alphabetical listing of the names, addresses, and phone numbers of all the people in an area who have phones and want their number to be listed. There is no charge to have your telephone number listed in the phone book, but some people prefer not to have their number listed. When a phone number is *unlisted*, you can't find it in the directory or get it from the operator.

It's important to know how to use the telephone directory. The directory has white pages that list the names of people and businesses who have phones. The yellow pages, in the back of the directory or in a separate book, list the names and numbers of businesses. They also have advertisements for some of the businesses listed. The yellow pages are classified alphabetically by *subject*. You can find a listing of plumbers, electricians, physicians, schools, and so on. Under each heading is an alphabetical listing of all the local businesses or people in that category.

White Pages

Gable, S. 321 Walton Av		225-3396
Garrod, Albert 1426 Maple Dr		446-5891
Gasten, Mark 686 Elmwood Av		454-6381
Gasten, Henry 687 Elmwood Av		454-6197
Geller, Nancy 459 Titus		645-6216
Glent, R.C. 566 Elm		425-7824
Gold, Seymour 455 Main		334-5872
Hallanhan, N. 366 Finn		746-0351
Holiday, Norman & Mary 263 Court		569-9023

Yellow Pages

RESTAURANTS

Mama's Pizzeria 425 Alexander	422-6891
Ming Hua 3982 Main	587-0034
Mindy's Salad Bowl 364 Elm Av	468-2342
Myron's Deli 2651 Ridge	536-8974
Northeast Inn 126 Lake Av	587-7772
O'Grady's 222 Sport	468-2399

Here is the kind of emergency information you would find in a telephone directory:

Basic Emergency Numbers

Ambulance Service	437-9804
Fire Department	433-8901
Police Department	232-5870
Poison Control	534-0624

Important: The numbers listed here are not real. You must look up the correct emergency phone numbers for the town or city you are in. They are different in each area of the United States.

The front of the phone book contains the phone numbers that may be needed in emergency situations. Before we continue, please look up and write down these phone numbers for your city in the space provided.

Police Department _____

Fire Department   _____

Poison Control   _____

Ambulance Service _____

For long-distance calls, you must dial either 1 or 0. One (1) is used if you call from a home telephone. Zero (0) is used if you call from a pay telephone or need the operator to assist you, as with a collect call. Next dial the three-digit area code for that city, then the person's seven-digit telephone number. If you need a phone number for someone who lives in another state or area code, dial 1, the appropriate area code, and then 555-1212.

Here are the area codes of some parts of the United States and Canada.

United States

California
  Los Angeles 213
  San Francisco 415
Colorado 303
District of Columbia 202
Florida
  Miami Beach 305
  Tampa 813
Michigan
  Detroit 313
New York
  Albany 518
  New York City
    Bronx, Manhattan 212
    Brooklyn, Queens,
    Staten Island 718
  Rochester 716

Pennsylvania
  Pittsburg 412
  Philadelphia 215
South Carolina 803
Texas
  Dallas 214
  Forth Worth 817
  Houston 713

Canada

Alberta 403
Ontario
  Ottawa 613
  Toronto 416
Quebec
  Montreal 514
  Quebec City 418

NOW YOU DO IT

Area Codes

The front of the phone book also provides information about making calls, when rates are the lowest, and what numbers to call to get information in various parts of the country. Look in the directory and write down the area code you would dial to reach the information operator to get the telephone number of someone in each of these cities:

131

United States	Canada
New York, New York 1 (　　　) 555-1212	Toronto, Ontario 1 (　　　) 555-1212
Los Angeles, California 1 (　　　) 555-1212	Quebec City, Quebec 1 (　　　) 555-1212
Fort Worth, Texas 1 (　　　) 555-1212	
Seattle, Washington 1 (　　　) 555-1212	
Denver, Colorado 1 (　　　) 555-1212	

Optional Activity: If you have a telephone book, do the following.

1. Find the chart in the front of the phone book that lists the telephone rates at different times of the day.

   When are the rates the cheapest? _____

   When are the rates the most expensive? _____

   Look up the rates to call each of the cities listed above. Use the most inexpensive rate.

2. Now use the directory to look up and write down the phone numbers of the following:

   Department of Motor Vehicles _____

   Immigration and Naturalization Services _____

   Main branch of the public library _____

3. Using the yellow pages of the directory, find a phone number for each of the following.

   A florist _____

   A TV repairman _____

   A dentist _____

   A pizza parlor _____

   An airline _____

4. Look up the name *Smith*. How many are there listed? _____

ANALYSIS

Names

Smith is a very common name in the United States.

The names listed in U.S. phone directories represent the countries all over the world that Americans come from. Here is a listing of some names. Can you identify their ethnic background? The answers on page 168.

Timothy O'Donnell _____

Samuel Rosenberg _____

Ahmad Hussain _____

Anthony Damiato _____

Ming Hua Huang _____

Demitrios Kostopoulos _____

Huynh Nguyen _____

Fritz Mann _____

Vladimir Shostov _____

The United States has often been called a giant "melting pot." It is the only country in the world that has people from so many different cultural and religious backgrounds.

LET'S SHARE

1. Do the names in your culture tell you something about people or their families? If you answer yes, write some names on the lines below and explain what a native of your country would know about the person upon learning his or her name.

_____

_____

_____

2. What name is very common in your language? _____ Look it up in the local phone book. Are there any people with that name living in your city? _____

NOW YOU DO IT

Here are some tasks to give you more practice in using the telephone. If you are in an English-speaking country, use an actual telephone to complete the task. If you are not, role-play these tasks with your instructor.

1. Call two airlines and ask them for the rate of a round-trip ticket to your favorite country. Explain that you want the cheapest flight, non-stop if possible.

   Airline _____ Cost _____

   Airline _____ Cost _____

2. Call the library and ask if it has books or records in your native language.
3. Call a local theater or concert hall and ask what is playing and the times. If possible, request a brochure on future events this season.
4. Call a florist and ask the cost of sending flowers to someone in a city where you have relatives or friends.
5. Call a stadium and ask what game is going to be played there this weekend.
6. Look up a movie in the newspaper. Call the theater and listen to the recorded message. Write down the information.

ROLE PLAY

Most of the time when you answer the telephone, you do not know who is calling or what they are going to say. In this exercise, you will have the freedom to decide the purpose of the call and to respond to the spontaneous conversation of your partner.

For example, if you call a doctor, you must decide on the purpose of your call. You might call to do any of these things:

Make an appointment
Ask what to do because you are sick
Cancel an appointment
Get the result of a blood test or a throat culture
Ask about your bill

The person you call, in this case a partner from class, will answer the phone and respond to what you say. However, your partner's response may not always be what you expect. For example, if you say, "This is Tanya Askanowski. I want to make an appointment," your partner might say, "Who? Please spell your name" or "Sorry, you have the wrong number" or "What is the appointment for?" Each of you must respond to what the other says. Let's practice using the example just given. Choose a partner. Decide who will make the phone call and who will answer the phone. Then begin the role playing with a call to the doctor.

Optional Activity: If a tape recorder is available, your teacher may want to tape some of the conversations. Later, the tapes may be played back to the class. The conversations may be discussed then in terms of content, appropriateness of responses, grammar, and comfort of the participants in speaking spontaneously. Use the rating sheet on page 136 for this activity.

Your teacher may also choose to have you work in a group of four instead of pairs. Two people will role-play while the other two act as observers. Observers should use the rating sheet on page 136.

Exercise

With a different partner, role-play each of the following calls. You may use one of the purposes given for the call or make up one of your own.

1. Call a friend:

   _____ to chat

   _____ to get the homework for one of your classes

   _____ to get someone's phone number

   _____ to make plans to go out

   _____ to extend an invitation to a party or social event

   _____ _____

2. Call a relative:

   _____ to chat

   _____ to wish him or her a happy birthday

   _____ to find out if their cold or other illness is better

   _____ to invite their family to dinner

   _____ _____

3. Call the library:

   _____ to find out what time they open and close

   _____ to find out if they have a particular book

   _____ to find out how to get a library card

   _____ to ask what the fines are for late books

   _____ _____

4. Call a classmate:

   _____ to ask when a test will take place

   _____ to ask for help with schoolwork

   _____ to ask if tomorrow is a holiday

   _____ _____

Conversation Rating Sheet

Circle the number that indicates how well you feel the conversational pair communicated. The lowest rating is 1, the highest 5.

1. The conversation was easy to understand.

   Not easy   1   2   3   4   5   Very easy

2. The responses to each other were appropriate.

   Not appropriate   1   2   3   4   5   Very appropriate

3. The participants seemed comfortable talking to each other.

   Uncomfortable   1   2   3   4   5   Very comfortable

4. The English they used was correct.

   Incorrect   1   2   3   4   5   Correct

5. They used appropriate idioms and phrases.

   Inappropriate   1   2   3   4   5   Appropriate

Going to
the Doctor

n some countries, medical care is free. People may visit the doctor, go to the hospital for surgery or tests, and receive medicine without paying. In the United States, health care is expensive. A visit to the doctor may cost from $25 to $250. Hospital care can be more than $200 per day. Because health care is so expensive, most people have health insurance. In this way, they pay a flat fee for individual or family coverage. The insurance company then pays all or part of their medical bills.

What system of health care exists in your country? How does it work?

In this chapter, we will discuss and practice common conversations that patients have while setting up appointments and when actually visiting the doctor's office. We will also discuss culture shock, symptoms of which appear in people who move to a new culture.

1 PREPARING FOR A VISIT TO THE DOCTOR

CHOOSING A DOCTOR

If you don't have a family doctor, now, while you're healthy, is the time to find one. The best way to find a good doctor is to ask friends to recommend one to you. Then call the doctor and make an appointment for a checkup. However, if no one can recommend a physician to you, call the American Medical Association in your area, listed in the telephone directory, and ask them to recommend a local doctor.

NOW YOU DO IT

With a partner, complete the following dialogue, in which you ask a friend to recommend a doctor to you. When you have finished, role-play your dialogue with a classmate.

You: _____

Friend: Well, I go to Dr. Susan Goddard. But across the street from your apartment building is a new doctor, Dr. Tai Lee. I've heard he is very good, also.

You: _____

Friend: I'm not sure about the telephone number, but you can find it in the yellow pages of the telephone directory under "physicians."

You: _____

Now write a dialogue in which you call the American Medical Association (AMA) and ask them to recommend a physician.

AMA: Hello. American Medical Association. Can I help you?

You: _____

AMA: What kind of doctor are you looking for? A general practitioner or a specialist?

You: _____

AMA: A general practitioner treats a variety of illnesses and will treat your whole family. A specialist concentrates in one area, like cardiology or dermatology.

You: _____

AMA: In that case, you may want to call Dr. Thomas McGee at 433-9874 or Dr. Roseanna Prater at 433-5370.

You: _____

AMA: If we can help you, please call again. Good-bye.

Put these conversations into practice by finding out the name of a doctor near where you live or to whom you already go and writing his or her name, address, and phone number below. When you get home, write this information near your telephone.

Doctor's name: _____

Address: _____

Telephone number: _____

ANALYSIS: SPECIALISTS

There are many different kinds of doctors, each specializing in a particular area of medicine. Can you match the doctor in the left column with the area in which the doctor specializes in the right column? Answers are on page 168.

_____ 1. Chiropodist

_____ 2. Pediatrician

_____ 3. Gynecologist

_____ 4. Obstetrician

_____ 5. Neurologist

_____ 6. Urologist

_____ 7. Orthodontist

_____ 8. Dentist

_____ 9. Veterinarian

_____ 10. Anesthesiologist

_____ 11. General practitioner (GP)

_____ 12. Internist

_____ 13. Orthopedist

_____ 14. Plastic surgeon

_____ 15. Ophthalmologist

A. A doctor who treats problems related to the nerves

B. A doctor who cares for teeth

C. A dentist who straightens teeth

D. A doctor who treats feet

E. A doctor who treats children only

F. A doctor who treats eye problems

G. A doctor who treats animals only

H. A doctor who treats urinary problems

I. A doctor who treats the entire family and who does not specialize in only one area

J. A doctor who treats problems of the glands

K. A doctor who performs cosmetic surgery

L. A doctor who treats women's problems

M. A doctor who cares for pregnant women

N. A doctor who puts patients to sleep prior to surgery

O. A doctor who treats bone problems

IDIOMS AND EXPRESSIONS

It is important to be able to describe properly the problem you are having to the doctor. To be accurate, you need to know the correct terminology. On the following page is a crossword puzzle of terms often used to describe illness. See how many you know. The answers are on page 168.

Across

1. A tightened muscle that causes pain
3. To cause pain by overstraining a joint
5. Pain in the belly
8. Causes pain on swallowing
11. Pain in the head
12. To throw up
13. Out of place (bone)
16. Feeling like the room is spinning
17. High body temperature
19. Illness caused by an influenza virus

Down

1. Unable to move one's bowels
2. Cracked or split (bone)
4. Pain in the ear
6. Feeling like you want to throw up
7. Hazy (vision)
9. Hole in a tooth
10. Loose and frequent bowel movements
14. Puffed up
15. Particular sensitivity to certain foods or medicines
18. Redness covering a portion of the skin
20. Pertaining to the nose

MODEL DIALOGUES

1. PERSON A: What's the matter? I heard you were sick.
   PERSON B: I feel awful. I have a headache, fever, and diarrhea.
   A: Do you feel dizzy?
   B: Yes, I am dizzy, too.

2. A: What happened to your knee? It looks swollen.
   B: I had an accident. I fell down the stairs.

3. A: Your eyes look puffy, and you sound nasal.
   B: I am allergic to cats.

LET'S SHARE

Every culture has "home remedies" for ailments and also superstitions about how to keep illness away. What do people in your culture do to alleviate suffering from these common illnesses?

Illness	In the United States	In Your Country
Cold	Take aspirin, lots of fluids, vitamin C; rest and keep warm.	
Flu	Take aspirin, liquids, vitamin C; rest and keep warm.	
Hiccups	Hold your breath and count to 10, drink a glass of water, or scare the person with hiccups.	
Headache	Take aspirin and rest.	
Diarrhea	Take clear liquids only; no solid food except toast or crackers.	
Swelling from an injury	Apply cold compresses (ice wrapped in a cloth).	

When you have finished, share your remedies with the class.

PHOTO ESSAY

What is happening in each of these photographs? Answers are on page 169.

A

B

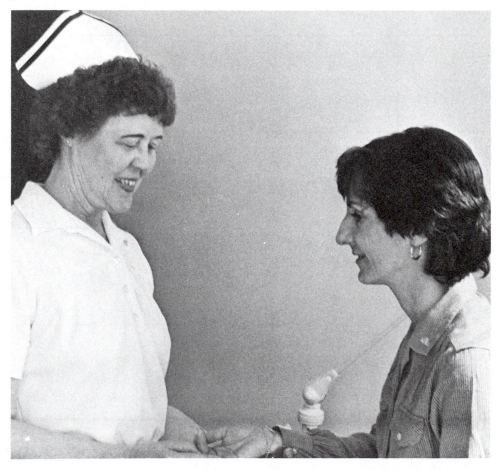

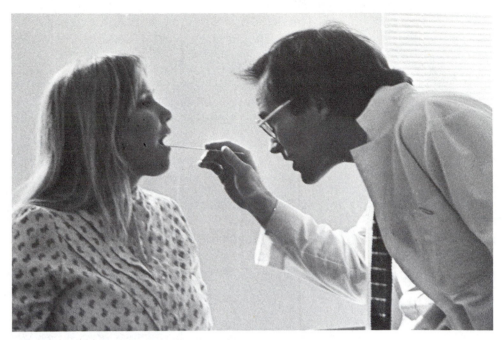

c

QUICK CUSTOMS QUIZ

Below are situations in which you might find yourself in the United States. Read each situation, decide what is appropriate, and choose the answer that best fits the circumstance. Draw a circle around the letter in front of your answer. Check your answers against those on page 169, which are the answers an American would probably give.

1. You are walking outside with some friends and step on a rusty nail. What should you do?

   a. Continue walking.
   b. Wash the wound and put a bandage on it.
   c. Call the doctor and ask if you need a tetanus shot.

2. You are in school, and your teacher has sent you to the school nurse because your eyes are red. The nurse thinks you have "pink eye" and calls your parent or guardian to take you home. What should you do?

   a. Rest that afternoon and then return to school.
   b. Go to the doctor.

3. You have a sore throat that has lasted for two weeks. What should you do?

   a. Go to the drugstore and ask for medicine.
   b. Gargle with salt water.
   c. Ignore it and it will go away.
   d. Go to the doctor.

4. The doctor puts you on penicillin and tells you to finish the medicine, which should last ten days. You feel fine after four days. What should you do?

   a. Take the medicine for ten days as the doctor said.
   b. Stop taking the medicine.
   c. Give the medicine to a friend who seems to have the same problem.

5. You have fallen and think you may have broken your leg. You are in great pain. It is 11 P.M. What should you do?

   a. Go to your doctor's house.
   b. Go to your doctor's office.
   c. Call the doctor at home.
   d. Call the doctor at his office.
   e. Go to the emergency room at the nearest hospital.
   f. Wait until morning to call or to go to the doctor's office.

6. The receptionist at the doctor's office gives you a bill for $40 for your office visit. You do not have $40. What should you do?

   a. Take the bill with you and pay later.
   b. Explain that you can't pay the bill.
   c. Tell her it is too expensive and ask her to charge you less.
   d. Go home and find a present to give the doctor instead of cash.
   e. Write a check even though you don't have the money to pay.
   f. Ask the receptionist to put the charge on your charge card.

7. You have not been feeling well and go to see the doctor. During the examination, he asks you some very personal questions about your life, for example: Do you have many friends? Do you go out socially? Do you lose your temper often? What is worrying you? When you are asked such questions, what should you do?

   a. Tell him it's none of his business.
   b. Answer his questions and ask him why he's asking them.
   c. Do not answer his questions.
   d. Respond politely.
   e. Tell him that you only came to him to take care of your physical problems.

8. You have a 3:30 P.M. appointment with the doctor. You arrive at his office at 3:25. It is now 4:15 and you are still sitting in the waiting room. What should you do?

   a. Get up and leave.
   b. Yell at the nurse or receptionist.
   c. Walk into the doctor's office.
   d. Continue to wait.
   e. Ask the receptionist how much longer the doctor will be.
   f. Find another doctor.

9. You have a doctor's appointment at 10:30 A.M. When you arrive, the office is very crowded. What should you do?

    a. Take a seat and wait for the nurse to call you.
    b. Leave because it appears you will have a long wait.
    c. Go up to the receptionist, give her your name, and take a seat.
    d. Come back later.

IDIOMS AND EXPRESSIONS

Here are some questions that the doctor may ask you when you visit his office and some questions that you may wish to ask your doctor.

Things the Doctor May Say to You

How long has this (illness, pain) been bothering you?
How long have you had this (sickness, pain, etc.)?
How long has this (the pain, illness, etc.) been going on?

Have you had this problem before? If so, when?

Where does it hurt?
Describe your pain.
Does it hurt when I press here?
What are your symptoms?

How did it (the accident) happen?
How did you hurt yourself?

Are you taking any medicine now?
What kind of medicine are you taking for the problem?
Are you allergic to any medicine?

Do you have insurance?
What kind of insurance do you have?
What is your insurance number?

Things the Doctor May Ask You to Do During the Examination

Say "ah." Stick out your tongue.
Open wide.
Hold your breath. Take a deep breath and hold it. Cough.
Now we're going to prick your finger for a blood sample. Give me your finger.
Breathe in deeply and let your breath out slowly.
Bend backward. Bend forward.

Things You May Say to the Doctor

What do you think is wrong?
What should I do about this (problem or illness)?
When will I be feeling better?
How should I take the medicine?
Is it (the illness) contagious?
Does the medicine have any side effects?
Do I need to come for another visit?
How long should I wait to call you if I don't feel better?

Before you go to see your doctor, it is a good idea to make a list of things that you want to ask. This way, you will not forget to ask about something that you have on your mind. Make sure that you answer and ask questions as specifically as possible. Be direct so that you can get the answers that you need. Don't feel shy about asking the doctor to repeat or to explain what he or she has said.

2 GOING TO THE DOCTOR

When patients arrive at the doctor's office, they should give their name to the receptionist, say which doctor they have an appointment to see, and wait in the reception room until their name is called. People usually sit one seat apart if possible and read the magazines provided in the reception room.

Each new patient is usually asked to fill out a Patient Health Form upon his or her first visit to the doctor. This form provides the doctor with information about a patient's past medical history.

On the following page is a sample health form. Fill it out by supplying the appropriate information. Look up any terms that are unfamiliar to you in a dictionary.

NOW YOU DO IT

The following conversations are typical of ones you would have if you visited a doctor in the United States. Notice that the doctor asks questions about the patient's physical and psychological health. Complete each conversation as carefully and realistically as possible.

1. You have a fever of 103 degrees Fahrenheit and a terrible sore throat. Call the doctor to make an appointment. It is important to know that doctors in the United States do not make house calls. You must go to their office when you are sick.

RECEPTIONIST: Hello, Dr. Brant's office.

You: _____

RECEPTIONIST: Please spell your name.

You: _____

RECEPTIONIST: What seems to be the problem, Mr. (Ms., Miss, Mrs.) _____?

You: _____

RECEPTIONIST: How long have you had this sore throat?

Continued on page 148

146

PATIENT HEALTH FORM

Name _____   Telephone (____) _____
                                             area code

Address _____
                        number & street

_____
        city   state   zip code

Person to contact in an emergency:

Name _____

Address _____

Telephone _____

Relationship to you _____

If you are covered by health insurance please indicate:

Name of the insurer _____

Address of insurer _____

Contract number _____

PERSONAL HISTORY: Please check (✔) if you have had any of the following medical problems.

_____ Scarlet fever	_____ Frequent headaches
_____ Measles	_____ Frequent colds
_____ German measles	_____ Hay fever, asthma
_____ Mumps	_____ Tuberculosis
_____ Poliomyelitis	_____ Back problems
_____ Malaria	_____ High blood pressure
_____ Ear, nose, and throat trouble	_____ Tumor, cancer, cyst
	_____ Stomach trouble
_____ Recurrent diarrhea	_____ Dizziness, fainting
_____ Kidney or urinary disease	_____ Diabetes

Are you allergic to any medicines? If so, what? _____

RECORD OF IMMUNIZATIONS

Please fill in date of latest immunization.

DT (Diphtheria, tetanus) _____
Polio (Sabin oral)   _____
Tuberculosis tests   _____
Measles   _____
Mumps   _____
Rubella (German measles) _____
Other vaccines   _____ _____ _____

Signature _____ Date _____

YOU: _____

RECEPTIONIST: What are you doing for it?

YOU: _____

RECEPTIONIST: I think you should have a throat culture. Can you come in at two-fifteen this afternoon?

YOU: _____

RECEPTIONIST: Ok. We'll see you then. Good-bye.

You arrive at the doctor's office at 2:15 P.M.

YOU: _____

NURSE: You've come for a throat culture.

YOU: _____

NURSE: Open wide and say "ah." (*swabs throat*) OK. Please call us after ten o'clock tomorrow morning for the results.

You call back at 10:00 A.M. the next day.

NURSE: Dr. Brant's office.

YOU: _____

NURSE: A throat culture?

YOU: _____

NURSE: Just a minute, Mr. (Ms., Miss, Mrs.) _____. That culture was positive. You have strep throat. Are you allergic to penicillin?

YOU: _____

NURSE: What druggist do you use?

YOU: _____

NURSE: Call and have the druggist call us for your prescription. You must take the medication for ten days and then come in for a throat culture two weeks later.

YOU: _____

NURSE: In a reculture, we culture your throat again to be sure the bacteria are gone.

YOU: _____

NURSE: If you have any trouble, please call us. You should be feeling better in about five days, but remember to take all ten days of the penicillin. I hope you feel better. Good-bye.

YOU: _____

2. You have come to see your doctor because you have the flu. Describe your symptoms.

DOCTOR: Hello, what seems to be the trouble?

YOU: _____

DOCTOR: I see. Are you vomiting?

YOU: _____

DOCTOR: Do you have a fever?

YOU: _____

DOCTOR: Let's take it and see what it is now.

YOU: _____

DOCTOR: You have 101 degrees. Have you had an upset stomach?

YOU: _____

DOCTOR: Any diarrhea?

YOU: _____

DOCTOR: How long has this been going on?

YOU: _____

DOCTOR: Do you feel dizzy at all?

YOU: _____

DOCTOR: OK. I'm going to check your ears. They seem to be OK. Open wide. Your throat's a little red. Let me feel your glands. Lift your chin a little bit. That's fine.
    Well, we have had quite a few cases of the flu lately. Take two aspirins every four hours, drink plenty of liquids, and get some rest. You should be up and around in a couple of days. I'll give you a prescription that should help you feel more comfortable. If you have any questions, call me.

YOU: _____

3. You have come to see your doctor because you have been feeling tired and generally disinterested in things for several weeks.

DOCTOR: Hello, I'm Dr. Phillips.

YOU: _____

DOCTOR: What seems to be the problem?

YOU: I don't know. I just feel tired all the time. I sleep all day. I'm not interested in studying or being with people.

DOCTOR: How long has this been going on?

YOU: _____

DOCTOR: Are there any other symptoms?

YOU: I'm just tired.

DOCTOR: Do you have friends?

YOU: _____

DOCTOR: Are you worried or upset about anything?

YOU: _____

DOCTOR: Has anything about your life changed?

YOU: _____

DOCTOR: How long have you lived in this city?

YOU: _____

DOCTOR: Hmm. Well, let's check you over. (*a few minutes later*) Well, I don't see anything physically wrong with you. Your heart is strong. Lungs are clear. Your blood count is good, blood pressure is in the normal range.

YOU: Then what seems to be troubling me?

DOCTOR: Sometimes when people move to a new location, especially a new country, they experience culture shock. Things that were easy to do in their own country, like traveling by bus, going shopping, and talking on the telephone, produce anxiety in a new country. Body language, gestures, idioms, foods, customs, socializing are all different. Becoming accustomed to these new ways is a strain. People experience tiredness from always having to think about how to do the simplest things. Sometimes this culture shock can become serious, and people become very depressed. I suggest you try to spend some time each week with people from your culture with whom you do not have to worry about how to act.

YOU: But my teachers say to speak English all the time.

DOCTOR: I understand, but right now we need to deal with your symptoms. Talk to people from your country, friends about some of the "funny" ways we Americans act and about some of the problems you have had. This will help you and them to feel better. Try to get out and do the things you enjoy.

YOU: How long does this usually last?

DOCTOR: Culture shock lasts for a while and then begins to disappear. The length of time varies from person to person. Be prepared to feel it again when you return home to your native country.

YOU: (*surprised*) _____

DOCTOR: When people reenter their native country, they again experience a cultural change. They must behave in ways that they have not thought about for a long time. They also find that because they have been away to another country, their friends and relatives treat them differently. This creates a shock to the body, and people may react again by withdrawing and sleeping a lot to get away from the strain.

YOU: _____

DOCTOR: If you aren't feeling better in two or three weeks, please call me.

150

Discussion Questions

1. What is culture shock?
2. Have you had any of the symptoms described or do you know anyone who has?
3. How did you or the other person feel? What did you do about it?

3 SIMULATION GAME: GOING TO THE DOCTOR*

You will have the opportunity to simulate a visit to a doctor and to try out the skills you have learned in this chapter. Try to gain as many points as possible during the playing period. Remember, to get points, you must express yourself correctly in English.

Setting Up the Game

To play this game, you will need the following:

1. *Personnel:* two doctors, a receptionist, a nurse
2. *Equipment:* One desk and chair for the doctor's office, a table for the examining table, several chairs for the waiting room, a desk, chair, and phone for the receptionist; medical forms for students to fill out. *Optional equipment:* blood pressure kit, thermometer, dressing robes, sheets, lab coats, etc.
3. *Setup:* Divide the room into three sections (or use three small rooms). In the first, set up a reception area with a desk and chair for the receptionist and chairs for waiting participants. On a small table, supply a number of magazines. In each of the other sections, set up an examining room. Use a table, preferably covered with a white sheet, for the examining table. (If you have a small class, you may need only one examining room.) You may use signs to label the receptionist's desk, reception area, examination room, and examination table.

POINT ACTIVITIES

In the Reception Area

1. Come into the office and give the receptionist your name.

   Point value: 1   Signature _____

*For detailed instructions, see the Appendix.

151

2. Ask the receptionist how long you will have to wait to see the doctor.

   Point value: 2   Signature _____

3. Fill out the form given to you by the receptionist.

   Point value: 2   Signature _____

4. Ask the receptionist to help you fill out a section of the form that you don't understand.

   Point value: 3   Signature _____

5. You have messed up your form and wish to begin again. Explain the situation to the receptionist and get another form.

   Point value: 4   Signature _____

6. You have been waiting for about 45 minutes. Explain to the receptionist that you have another appointment, and make another appointment to see the doctor later in the week.

   Point value: 4   Signature _____

7. Ask another patient in the waiting room what time it is.

   Point value: 2   Signature _____

8. Ask another patient in the reception area where the rest room is.

   Point value: 3   Signature _____

9. Make small talk with someone in the reception area for three minutes.

   Point value: 3   Signature _____

10. Ask a friend who accompanied you to the doctor to recommend a doctor who treats skin rashes.

    Point value: 2   Signature _____

In the Examining Room

11. Explain to the nurse the nature of your illness.

    Point value: 4   Signature _____

12. Ask the nurse to explain what will happen during the examination. Have the nurse go into detail about at least one procedure (blood pressure, laboratory tests, etc.).

    Point value: 4   Signature _____

13. Ask the nurse one question about your illness.

    Point value: 2   Signature _____

14. Ask the nurse what your temperature or blood pressure is.

    Point value: 1   Signature _____

15. Tell the doctor about your symptoms.

    Point value: 3   Signature ⸻

16. Answer the doctor's questions about yourself and your illness.

    Point value: 4   Signature ⸻

17. Ask the doctor when you will be feeling better.

    Point value: 1   Signature ⸻

18. Ask the doctor what you should do and what medicine you should take.

    Point value: 3   Signature ⸻

19. Ask the doctor exactly what the side effects of the medicine are and what you should or should not do or eat while taking the medicine.

    Point value: 4   Signature ⸻

20. Ask the doctor a question about a personal problem you are having at home.

    Point value: 4   Signature ⸻

21. Ask the doctor to tell you about the kind of illness you have—what causes it, is it contagious, how long will it last, is it serious?

    Point value: 5   Signature ⸻

22. Ask the doctor when you should come again to his office or when you should call him if you are not feeling better.

    Point value: 1   Signature ⸻

In the Reception Room After Seeing the Doctor

23. Ask the receptionist for another appointment with the doctor for next week. Ask her to write down the date and time for you.

    Point value: 2   Signature ⸻

24. Ask the receptionist about paying your bill.

    Point value: 1   Signature ⸻

25. Ask the receptionist to submit a claim for the doctor's visit to your insurance company. Answer her questions carefully.

    Point value: 3   Signature ⸻

26. Tell the receptionist that you cannot pay your bill during the visit but would like to make arrangements to pay it later. Ask her how to do this.

    Point value: 3   Signature ⸻

Appendix

Simulation Game Directions

1 FACILITATOR'S DIRECTIONS

The four simulation games are designed to acquaint international students with American customs and culture by involving them in activities that simulate actual situations. The games are designed for use with specific chapters of *Culturally Speaking* so that students will have the opportunity to use the language skills they have acquired. By working through the different games, students will learn and use new skills in English conversation, meet and interact with other students and facilitators, and become familiar with American customs.

The atmosphere should be light, one that will encourage participation and enjoyment of the game. Prizes should be given only as an encouragement, never as a "contest." If possible, each participant should "win" something, although it is permissible, of course, to give prizes of different values. One successful approach is to display all the prizes before the game and then let each winner choose one. Another approach is not to use prizes at all but simply to enjoy the game and the interaction.

SETUP

Each game has complete directions for setup, supplies, facilitators, and questions. The layout formats are only suggestions and can be changed to suit the needs and size of the group. Make the effort to give the setup a realistic feeling.

154

Supplies

Before the game begins, make certain to have all supplies organized and "ready to go." Paper money, coins, credit cards, checks, and identification (if required) can be hand-made.

Be sure to label any items that students bring in for use in a simulation game. Students should replace items used for props (for example, clothing in the clothing store) when they finish their activity rather than wait until the end of the game. This will assure an adequate supply of materials for all game participants.

Objective

In each simulation game, students use the game pages in the book to complete game activities. For each game, there is a list of activities to be completed. Each activity has a different value, depending on its level of difficulty. Students are given time to look over the activities and determine which ones they wish to attempt. Students should then be told that when they complete an activity, they must get the signature of the person who participated with them. Sometimes this person will be a classmate and sometimes a facilitator.

Students should be told how much time they will have to participate in the activity and that the person who gets the most points at the end is the "winner." Playing time is usually 20 minutes.

Some students will become very active; others may be more reluctant. As with any game, the more adept the players (in this case, those who are more proficient in the language), the easier it is to acquire points. For this reason, a chance element has been incorporated in each game. You will notice that there are some activities that can be initiated only by the facilitator. Therefore, the teacher may assist a shy student or a student less proficient in the language by initiating an activity.

At the end of the playing time, students should be told to stop. Depending on the students you are working with, you may have them total their own scores, have them exchange game pages and tally them for each other, or have a committee collect and tally the pages.

FACILITATORS

The instructor is generally the main facilitator. Sometimes teachers combine classes, affording the group two facilitators. The number of facilitators required depends on the size of the group. We suggest one facilitator for a group of 20, two for 30, three for 40 students. Advanced students may assist as facilitators.

Individuals who facilitate games should be thoroughly trained for their roles or have lived in an English-speaking country so that they can approximate the behavior students would experience in the real world. For example, salespeople should be helpful (offer assistance, make suggestions) but should be allowed to be pushy or rude or to ignore participants. Cashiers should request correct identification, look up credit cards on a "hot sheet," and even make mistakes with change. Salespeople should make a participant produce a receipt for a returned item and demand an explanation rather than simply accept the return or exchange without a struggle.

Most important, facilitators should not sign for an activity unless the participant uses comprehensible, reasonably correct English. However, they may prompt students, if necessary. Remember, this game's purpose is to simulate situations the students will have to face and to give them the opportunity to use and to sharpen their English skills.

Facilitators should also control the flow of the game by encouraging students to participate. Shy students can be drawn into the action by facilitators who ask them questions to encourage their participation. It is crucial, however, that students not be allowed to speed through activities by saying, "I'll sign for you if you sign for me." The emphasis should be on having a good time, getting to know one another, and learning English rather than on competition and speed.

One option is to have students tape-record their interactions. These tapes could be transcribed, reviewed, and discussed at a later session.

TIME

The length of the game segments depends on the number of players and the complexity of the activity. Generally speaking, most games should be concluded in around 45 to 50 minutes: 20 minutes playing time, 10 minutes discussion and tally, 10 minutes for giving out prizes and cleaning up. The nightclub game, because of its complexity and emphasis on social activities, can run longer. All games are designed for use within the ESL class and to fall within a standard class period.

SPECIAL CONSIDERATIONS

Before beginning a game, facilitators should have students assemble the material they will need for the game. Students will also need a pen or pencil. If the game is being used in an orientation program, do not supply the students with name tags. The purpose of the game is to get students to interact with each other.

Starting to Play

Have some students set up the room using the instructions in the book while others begin reading the directions on page 157.

Then carefully explain the objective of the game. Outline the rules, especially about signing when someone has completed an activity. Let the students know that this is an activity to be enjoyed, not a competition to get points. The prizes are offered only to make things more interesting, not as a justification to rush from one activity to another. Let the students look over the activities and become aware that they may choose the activities they wish to participate in; however, they may have to follow a sequence (for example, you cannot complain about your food to the waitress until she brings it, and she cannot bring it until you order it). After explaining the game, ask for questions and give a hypothetical example of situations that may occur during the game to let the students know what to expect and what is expected of them.

Before beginning the game, give the students time to read the activities and select the ones they want to do. They should complete as many tasks as they wish but may not repeat any for credit. Remind them that some activities are worth more than others.

Since interaction is extremely important, groups should contain at least ten participants, if possible, but (except for the nightclub game) not more than 20. The number of facilitators varies according to group size and roles in a game.

Feedback Session

The feedback session, which should take place immediately after the game, is a critical part of the learning experience. Participants should discuss what happened, their feelings and experiences, and how they handled various situations. It is important to discuss problems as well as triumphs and to provide alternative ways to deal with game situations.

Questions for discussion may include:
1. How did you feel when you played the game?
2. What was the most difficult part for you to do? Why was this hard for you?
3. What was the easiest thing to do? Why?
4. What activities did you do in this game that are different from those you would do in your own culture?
5. What would you have done differently in the game? What would you have said or done?
6. What activity would you add to the game? Why?

2 STUDENTS' DIRECTIONS

OBJECTIVE

The simulation games are designed to simulate or imitate situations that you will encounter in the real world. The purpose of a simulation game is for the players (participants) to practice an activity that they may someday have to do outside the classroom.

In this game, you will apply the English you have studied to situations such as eating out, shopping, visiting the doctor, and participating in a classroom.

DIRECTIONS

1. There are four simulation games in your book: Attending School (page 36), Going to a Nightclub (page 101), Shopping in the United States (page 114), and Going to the Doctor (page 151).
2. Read the list of activities you may choose to do. Note that you may do some or all of the items listed. Note also that some activities must be done in order; for example, in the nightclub, you must ask for a menu before you can order.
3. Each activity is assigned a point value. Activities that are harder to do culturally or require more advanced English receive more points.
4. Decide which activities you would like to do. When the teacher tells you to start, begin working on the activities.
5. Each activity requires you to speak to someone. When you complete an activity, ask the person you spoke with to sign your sheet after the activity you have completed. Only the person who begins the activity gets the points. At the end of the game, the items for which you obtained signatures are added to give you a total score.

MENU

Appetizers

Chicken Wings	1.25
Grapefruit Half	1.00
Shrimp Cocktail	2.75

Soups

Chicken Noodle	1.00
Clam Chowder	1.50
Soup du Jour	1.25

Entrees

Southern Fried Chicken	6.00
Spaghetti with Meatballs	5.50
Roast Beef au Jus	11.00
Lamb Chops	12.00
Filet of Sole	8.00

Entrees come with tossed salad, bread, baked potato or french-fried potatoes and vegetable.

Desserts

Chocolate Cake	2.00
Apple or Cherry Pie	1.50
Southern Pecan Pie	1.75
Ice Cream	1.00
Chocolate or Vanilla Pudding	1.00

Beverages

Soda	.75
Coffee or Tea	.75
Milk	1.00
Fruit Juice	1.25

Answers

CHAPTER ONE

A

B

MATCHING (page 3)

A. 4 D. 1
B. 5 E. 2
C. 3

HAND GESTURE IDIOMS (page 4)

1. I 4. B 7. D
2. F 5. C 8. A
3. G 6. H 9. E

QUICK CUSTOMS QUIZ (page 7)

1. a. She shows her excitement by her smile and open nonverbal cues like open, uplifted clenched fists.
2. a, b, c. This gesture, which is used primarily by children, has many meanings, all negative.

3. b. A shoulder shrug indicates that a person does not know the answer to a question.
4. c. Notice that the person is resting his head on his hand and shows intense concentration by his serious facial expression.
5. a. She shows surprise by placing her hand on her forehead, opening her mouth, and widening her eyes.

GESTURE IDIOMS (page 8)

1. L	4. H	7. B	10. J
2. A	5. G	8. C	11. K
3. D	6. F	9. E	12. I

PHOTOANALYSIS (page 9)

1. They appear to know each other well. They are touching each other, smiling, and maintaining eye contact. For Americans, they are standing close to one another, which indicates that they may know each other very well.

2. The woman on the left is talking and explaining. You can tell this by her open gestures (reaching out, palms up) and widely open eyes. The woman on the right is surprised or shocked. You can tell this by her expression and her hand over her mouth.

3. The man is talking, and the girls are interested in what he is saying. The girls are leaning toward him, looking directly at him, and paying attention.

4. *Photo A:* The man and woman are angry at each other. She looks very stern and has her arms folded over her chest. The man is standing very straight and is gripping his hands tightly, which may indicate he is making a request. He is frowning also.

   Photo B: Another man seems to be trying to explain the situation. You can tell by his open-handed gesture. Both people are looking at the speaker, indicating that they are paying attention to what he is saying.

   Photo C: Apparently, the person who was attempting to clarify the situation said something amusing. The younger man found it very funny. The woman appears to be trying to prevent herself from laughing.

OBSERVING (page 13)

2. At least one seat apart if possible.
3. At least 2 feet apart or more if possible. People do not touch or shove.
4. At least one seat apart if possible. People generally do not speak to other people in a restaurant unless they know them.
5. 3 to 4 feet
6. 2 to 3 feet

7. As close as 18 inches (1½ feet)
8. 3 to 4 feet
9. 3 to 4 feet unless you know the child well. People do not touch or kiss unless they are members of the family.

CHAPTER TWO

QUICK CUSTOMS QUIZ (page 25)

1. c. It is always best to smile and call your teacher by name rather than "teacher."
2. a. In the United States, it is considered respectful and correct to look directly into the eyes of the person who is talking to you regardless of that person's position. To look away would seem very impolite to an American and would show that you are not interested or that you lack respect.
3. a or b. Depending on the size of the class and the difficulty of the problem, you may either ask for a clarification during the class or see the instructor after class for help.
4. a. Call your adviser. Explain your illness and make another appointment for when you are feeling better.
5. c or d. Depending on your course requirements and class load, you should either make arrangements with your adviser to drop the class with the instructor's permission or ask the instructor for permission to finish the class work during the next semester.
6. d. Attending class, even if the teacher doesn't seem to like you, is very important in the United States. Work as hard as you can, and make the most of the class. Speaking to a guidance counselor may help you feel better, but neither he nor your parents can make the teacher change your grade.
7. a or c. Class participation is very important in the United States. However, if you feel uncomfortable, discuss your feeling with your instructor.
8. c. Covering your paper will let the other person know that you do not approve of his or her cheating. Do not allow anyone to copy your work, because this makes you guilty of cheating too!
9. c. Discuss your questions with your teacher privately. Do not ask about the interpretation of grades or answers during the class period.
10. a. It is considered correct to volunteer to answer questions. However, do not try to be the one to answer questions all the time. Let other students have the opportunity to answer also.
11. a or d. Most teachers are very reasonable and are generally willing to test students at different times if they have a good reason to do so.

IDIOMS (page 30)

1. L	5. B	8. H	11. F
2. E	6. I	9. C	12. K
3. A	7. J	10. G	13. M
4. D			

CHAPTER THREE

IDIOMS (page 41)

1. Someone who is your friend when you have no problems but who disappears when you need help
2. An adult female friend of a gentleman or another lady
3. Someone of the opposite sex whom you are seeing regularly to the exclusion of anyone else
4. Extremely good friends; derives from a children's ritual whereby good friends sometimes prick their finger and mix a bit of their blood
5. People who are alike usually form friendships.
6. One person who is not nice is a bad influence on the people he or she spends time with.
7. Someone who helps you when you need it is a true friend.
8. People who spend too much time together grow to dislike each other.

QUICK CUSTOMS QUIZ (page 55)

1. c. Politely ask the person to turn down his stereo and give your reasons. If he will not cooperate, then call the housing authorities or the police to make a complaint (e or f).
2. b. Politely but firmly refuse. You don't need to justify your decision or apologize.
3. b. You may get into trouble if you allow others to copy your work, and the other person will not learn to work the problems. If someone needs help, you may show them your class notes or teach them to solve the problems, but you should not let them copy your work.
4. e. It's generally better to tell someone how you feel and try to work out a solution together before you go to the housing authorities.
5. a. Your friend is offering to introduce you and arrange a date for you (fix you up) with someone whom he knows. You do not know the person and therefore are relying on your friend's judgment (blind date). There is no obligation to continue the relationship beyond the first date unless both of you wish to.

CHAPTER FOUR

IDIOMS AND EXPRESSIONS (page 61)

1. H	5. I	9. D	13. A
2. F	6. J	10. G	14. C
3. L	7. K	11. N	
4. M	8. B	12. E	

QUICK CUSTOMS QUIZ (page 62)

1. c. By smiling, you are indicating that you would like to meet him. His smile means that he would like to get to know you and should not be considered bold or rude.

2. e. Catching a person's eye and smiling is the best way to show your interest. If the other person wishes to meet you also, he or she will smile back. Actions described in a, b, and c would be considered shocking or offensive to an American.

3. a. Generally speaking, this phrase is a euphemism for asking a person's consent to have sex. If one accompanies another person to an apartment or home under these circumstances, one is tacitly agreeing to engage in physical intimacy.

4. a, b, c, d. These are acceptable forms of public affection; passionate kissing is never acceptable.

5. all

6. b. If one is attending a prom, the man should bring the woman a corsage or flowers. The woman may give her date a flower for his buttonhole, usually a rose or carnation to match her dress.

7. c. If the man asks the woman out, he should pay the expenses unless they agree to share the expenses before the date. Should the woman ask the man out, she pays for all expenses. The man may pay the tips for dinner or taxis if he wishes, however. If the man or woman are uncomfortable having someone pay for their expenses they may suggest splitting the costs.

8. b. Generally speaking, the man picks up the woman at her home unless they agree to meet at another location for the sake of mutual convenience.

CHAPTER FIVE

RIDDLES (page 69)

1. A garbage truck
2. A table
3. A teapot
4. A newspaper
5. A pink car-nation

CHAPTER SIX

ANALYSIS (page 85)

A. Independence Day
B. Thanksgiving
C. Easter
D. Halloween
E. Christmas

GREETING CARDS: MATCHING (page 86)

1. B	3. A	5. G	7. E
2. C	4. D	6. F	8. H

MATCHING (page 88)

1. H	5. J	9. I	13. A
2. E	6. L	10. G	14. N
3. C	7. K	11. B	15. P
4. M	8. F	12. D	16. O

QUICK CUSTOMS QUIZ (page 90)

1. a or b. When an adult is invited to a dinner party, it is considered polite to bring a small, relatively inexpensive gift for the hostess, such as a bottle of wine or a box of candy. Unless asked, don't bring food. If you are invited to a potluck dinner, however, you should bring a dish of food large enough to feed the whole group. The hostess will usually tell you what type of dish to bring. Don't bring a friend or a relative to dinner unless the host or hostess has told you that you may do so. Unless children have been specifically invited, do not bring them, especially to evening social functions.

2. a. Generally speaking, when you are not eating, you should place your hands in your lap, although in very casual situations, you may place your hands and wrists on the table.

3. b, c, e, g.

4. a, e. Carrying on a conversation is an important part of dining in the United States. It is important to let your host know you are enjoying the food by commenting on it verbally, not by burping, smacking your lips, or making any other noises.

5. b. The host (or hostess) will ask you if you want a second portion (seconds). If you wish to eat more, thank the host, comment on the food, and take a second helping the first time it is offered. Often the host will ask if you wish to have the last piece of meat or helping from a dish (this is considered polite in the United States). If you refuse, the host will assume that you do not want to eat any more and will not ask you again.

    If you are in a very casual situation, such as a picnic or family gathering, you may ask for seconds when you want more. Simply say, "Please pass me the (*food*). Thank you."

6. c. This is a way to make pleasant conversation but not necessarily an offer to have dinner. If the offer is ultimately taken up, each person is expected to pay for his or her own dinner.

7. b. This is often a pleasantry that people use on parting, not a specific invitation. In the United States, always call or make arrangements before you go to visit anyone.

8. b. The woman goes first and is followed by the man, who helps her off with her coat, holds all doors, and pulls out her chair at the table for her to be seated.

9. c. The other behaviors would either amuse or irritate other restaurant patrons and your waiter.
10. a, c, d. Each state has a legal drinking age, generally between 18 and 21. Since the restaurant or bar must check to see if you are old enough to be served liquor, you must show a piece of identification that has your birth date on it.
11. a, sometimes c or e. Cash is always acceptable and generally preferred. Although more expensive restaurants accept credit cards (Visa, American Express, MasterCard), "family" and "fast food" restaurants like McDonald's, Burger King, and Taco Bell will not. Restaurants will often accept traveler's checks but never personal checks or currencies of other countries.
12. b. Tell the waiter that your check is incorrect and ask him to correct it. Because there is an unwritten rule in the United States that "the customer is always right," businesses strive to please the customer.

ANALYSIS (page 94)

1. Early or on time	5. On time	9. On time
2. Early or on time	6. Early	10. On time
3. On time	7. Early	11. On time
4. On time	8. Early	12. On time

CHAPTER SEVEN

MATCHING (page 105)

1. E	4. K	7. H	10. J
2. F	5. B	8. L	11. I
3. D	6. C	9. G	12. A

QUICK CUSTOMS QUIZ (page 107)

1. c. Americans often browse, and it is perfectly all right to tell the clerk politely that you are just looking.
2. c. To receive the discount, you must purchase the product and give the clerk the coupon when you pay for the item. The amount of the coupon will be deducted from your bill.
3. a or d. Since prices in American stores are fixed, you cannot bargain for a better price but must pay the amount on the ticket. The only exceptions are articles sold by individuals (used goods) or large articles like automobiles and large appliances.
4. a or c. The accompanying chart will help you know your size in the United States.
5. e. Although you can return a garment if it doesn't fit, you can save yourself a lot of time by trying it on in the fitting room before you buy

it. Trying a garment on in the store under or over your clothes or taking it to a rest room to try on could get you arrested for shoplifting (stealing).

6. a, b, d, e. All of these are good ideas, especially e. The warranty should specifically state what the car dealership will pay for if repairs are needed and how long the car is covered under the terms of the warranty. Ask questions and make sure you understand the terms and the answers.

Clothing Size Conversion Chart

Children's Dresses and Suits

American	2	4	6	8	10	12
European	40–45	50–55	60–65	70–75	80–85	90–95

Women's Clothing

American	6	8	10	12	14	
European	36	38	40	42	44	

Men's Suits and Overcoats

American	36	38	40	42	44	46
European	46	48	50	52	54	56

Women's Shoes

American	4	5	6	7	8	9
European	34	35	36	37	38	39

Men's Shoes

American	7	8	9	10	11	12
European	40	41	42	43	44	45

Men's Shirts

American	14	14½	15	15½	16	16½
European	36	37	38	39	41	42

QUICK CUSTOMS QUIZ (page 110)

1. e. Most stores will not allow returns or refunds after seven days. In this situation, it is best to thank the clerk and leave if you cannot convince him to allow you to return the item.

2. b. Most stores will allow you to make an even exchange by letting you substitute an item in a different size or color. They may even allow you to use the purchase price of the item as partial payment for another item. Unless you have a dated sales receipt that shows that the buyer paid cash, you cannot get a cash refund.

3. b. New appliances are covered under warranty, which means that the manufacturer will replace or repair the appliance if anything goes wrong within a stated period of normal use. Keep the warranty and make certain that you understand it.

4. a. Unordered merchandise may be kept, but you should notify the company of the error.

5. c. It is extremely important that you return the applesauce and jar with the glass to the store so that they may remove all the applesauce that was bottled by that company from the shelves. Otherwise, someone may be injured by eating the defective applesauce. In exchange for a product returned under such conditions, the company will replace the product and sometimes give the customer additional packages of the product free.

CHAPTER EIGHT

MATCHING (page 117)

1. M	5. G	9. J	13. D
2. E	6. F	10. H	14. C
3. L	7. I	11. A	
4. B	8. K	12. N	

QUICK CUSTOMS QUIZ (page 122)

1. c, then b. If you feel that a mistake has been made in your bill, you may call the business office and ask them to check your account. If they find no evidence that you have paid, you should either send them or take to them in person proof that you did pay the bill.

2. c. When someone dials the wrong number, it is polite to say, "I'm sorry. You have the wrong number." Generally, the person will apologize and hang up. Sometimes people ask for your number. It is better to ask what number they were trying to dial than to give out your number. They generally ask this question to find out how the mistake was made (did they misdial, or is the number they have incorrect?).

3. b, then e. If you reach a wrong number on a long-distance call, you should call the operator and tell her that you got the wrong number. If you do this, the phone company will not charge you for the call.

4. c. The receptionist probably had to answer another call. She has asked you to hold the phone and wait until she can speak with you. This usually only takes a few minutes and is not meant to seem impolite. When she returns to the line, she will probably say, "Thank you for holding. Can I help you?" or "I'm sorry to keep you waiting." If you are in a hurry and cannot wait even a short while, hang up and call back later.

5. b. Once in a while, people who are carrying on a conversation get "cut off" (something happens that disconnects their call). If this happens, hang up and either wait for the person to call you back or call him. (Ordinarily, the person who placed the call the first time calls again.)

6. a, later f. The telephone company suggests that if you get nuisance calls, hang up. Never talk to these people or give them any informa-

tion. Sometimes they just dial a number at random and don't even know what number they've called. If they continue to phone you, call the phone company and register a complaint.

7. b. Airlines, doctor's offices, and other places of business that receive many calls use taped messages to tell people they are busy and to ask them to hold the phone. To make the caller feel more comfortable and relaxed, they sometimes play music until someone can answer the phone. Stay on the phone and wait.

8. c. More and more places of business and even homes are using tape recorders to play and record phone messages. When you hear a taped message, listen carefully for the message, wait for the beeping sound, and then give your name, telephone number, and any other important information. Be sure to speak slowly and to keep your message short.

9. b. The operator will bill your home phone instead of the phone you are using to make the call or the phone whose number you are calling.

10. a or b. This is a call in which the person calling tells the operator to charge the call to the people who are receiving the call. The operator always asks the person receiving if he or she will accept the charges (pay for the call). If the reply is no, the call cannot be made.

11. c. An operator or tape recording will tell you this if the person you are calling has had the phone disconnected for a while. People sometimes do this when they go on vacation. It can also mean that there are some mechanical problems with the phone or that the telephone company has disconnected the phone.

12. a. The operator or a recording will say this to indicate that you do not need help to complete the call (and consequently can avoid paying for the call at the higher operator-assisted rate).

ANALYSIS: NAMES (page 133)

Irish, Jewish, Arabic, Italian, Chinese, Greek, Vietnamese, German, Russian

CHAPTER NINE

ANALYSIS: SPECIALISTS (page 139)

1. D	5. A	9. G	13. O
2. E	6. H	10. N	14. K
3. L	7. C	11. I	15. F
4. M	8. B	12. J	

CROSSWORD PUZZLE SOLUTION (page 140)

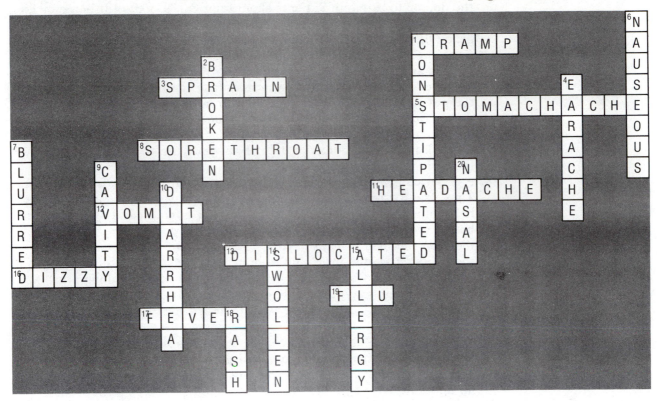

PHOTO ESSAY (page 142)

A. People are waiting in a doctor's waiting room.
B. A nurse is preparing to take a patient's pulse.
C. A doctor is examining a patient.

QUICK CUSTOMS QUIZ (page 143)

1. b, then c. With a puncture wound, it is best to call a doctor. This type of wound may require a tetanus shot to prevent a more serious illness.
2. b. If you are sent home with a contagious illness, either you must wait until you are completely well, as with a sore throat or the flu, or seek medical help to combat the illness.
3. d. Most sore throats go away within a few days. A persistent sore throat should be "cultured" for the presence of streptococcus ("strep") infection. Without proper treatment, this can lead to dangerous illness.
4. a. Patients should always follow the doctor's directions exactly. If they experience any problems as a result of the medication, they should call the doctor immediately. No prescription medicine should be given to anyone else.
5. e. Most doctors' offices are open Monday through Friday from 9 A.M. to 5 P.M. Generally, if you call when the office is closed, a recording will

give you a number to call. Call that number and leave a message for the doctor to call you. Patients should not call a doctor at home or go to the doctor's office for assistance when the office is closed. An emergency like a suspected broken leg requires X-rays and immediate attention. The patient should go to the nearest hospital emergency room.

6. a. Bills are presented at the time of treatment. Although you are encouraged to pay at this time, you may take the bill with you and mail the payment later. Doctors generally do not accept charge cards.

7. d. American doctors believe that a person's life-style and personality have a great deal to do with their physical health. For this reason, doctors ask many questions not only about your health but about your life-style and feelings.

8. e. Americans are accustomed to being kept waiting in a doctor's office. They usually arrive on time, however. If kept waiting for more than a half hour, they politely ask the receptionist how much longer it will be before they see the doctor. When they see the doctor, they may politely mention the long wait by saying, "You must have been very busy today" or "I waited over half an hour to see you." Most doctors try not to keep patients waiting, but it is difficult to know how long a patient's problem may take to diagnose and treat. American doctors are generally interested in talking with their patients to understand the total problem.

9. c. Whenever you go to an office, whether it's a doctor's, dentist's, college, or employment office, you must go up to the receptionist, greet her, and give her your name. You must do this even though you have an appointment.

Glossary

acquaintance (n) A person you know or have met. Such people are not usually considered friends because you do not know them well.

Although he lives next door, I don't know him well. He is just an *acquaintance.*

all right (adv) Acceptable, OK, truly.

It is *all right* with me if you finish the test tomorrow.
We will find out the test results tomorrow, *all right!*

American Medical Association (AMA) (n) The medical association to which most doctors in the United States belong.

Most American doctors are members of the *AMA.*

anniversary (n) An occasion celebrated to honor each year that people have been married.

A twenty-fifth wedding *anniversary* is called the silver anniversary.

anxiety (n) Fear or nervousness about something.

I have a great deal of *anxiety* about taking tests.

apologize (v) To say that one is sorry.

People usually *apologize* when they do something wrong.

baby shower (n) A party given by the friends or family of a woman who will soon have a baby.

Mary Ann received many presents for the baby at her surprise *baby shower.*

bargain (n) Something that costs less than it usually should or less than you expected to pay.

I bought this beautiful wool coat for only $50! It is a real *bargain!*

beef patty (n) A hamburger without the roll.

I just want a *beef patty.* I'm on a diet.

beep (n) A short, high-pitched sound.

At the sound of the *beep,* please leave your name and message.

blind date (n) An arrangement, made by a friend, for two people who do not know each other to go out together.

Thomas had a good time on his *blind date,* though he had been hesitant about going.

B.O. (n) Body odor.

His *body odor* was so strong that people began to leave the room.

body language (n) Gestures; the movements of the face, hands, and body that add expression to one's speech or reveal one's attitude or feelings about a person or situation.

His *body language*—crossed arms—said that he didn't agree with what the speaker was saying.

bother (n) An irritation.

Driving to the airport at night is a real *bother*.

bother (v) To annoy.

The loud music in the next room *bothered* him.

bowling (n) An indoor game in which people throw a large, heavy ball to knock down ten wooden pins.

Let's go *bowling* this Saturday night.

brand (n) The specific name given to a manufactured product.

There are many *brands* of shampoo.

bridal shower (n) A party given by the friends of a woman who is going to be married.

Twenty friends attended June's *bridal shower*.

bride (n) A woman who is getting married.

Doesn't the *bride* look lovely in her gown!

browse (v) To look at things in a store without intending to buy anything.

When I was *browsing*, I saw several dresses I would like to buy when I get the money.

buddy (n) A very good friend; sometimes used ironically to show anger.

This is my *buddy*, Jim, whom I grew up with.

Look, *buddy*, why don't you keep your mouth shut!

cabbie (n) A person who drives a taxi.

The *cabbie* told him the fare to the airport would be $12.00.

catch someone's eye (v) To look at someone briefly at the same time as that person is looking at you; to get someone's attention.

It took me five minutes to *catch the waiter's eye*.

chapel (n) A place where people hold religious services, including weddings and funerals.

Funeral services will be in the *chapel* at 4 P.M.

checkup (n) A complete physical examination given when a patient is healthy to be certain that the patient is in good health.

Physicians recommend a yearly *checkup* for everyone over 50.

confide in (someone) (v) To tell someone something that you would not tell anyone else.

When I had problems with my family, I *confided in* my teacher.

credit (a call) (v) Not to be charged for a call you have made on the telephone.

The operator *credited* the call because I got the wrong number.

culture (n) 1. The society in which one lives.

Each person is a product of his or her native *culture*.

2. The growth and examination, under laboratory conditions, of a sample of bacteria taken from a person's body.

The doctor took a *culture* to see what kind of bacteria were causing his sore throat.

culture shock (n) A feeling of uneasiness which comes as a result of living in a country where the rules of behavior are different from one's native country.

All people experience *culture shock* to some degree.

dandruff (n) Dry flakes of the skin of the scalp that fall from one's hair onto one's shoulders.

He should use a special shampoo to get rid of his *dandruff*.

date (n) A social, usually romantic occasion spent with someone of the opposite sex.

Do you have a *date* this Saturday night?

date (v) To go on a date or dates.

I would really like to *date* Terry.

James and Julia have been *dating* for six months.

dating service (n) An organization that arranges dates for people for a fee.

Some Americans use a *dating service* to help them meet people of the opposite sex.

daydreaming (n) Not paying attention to what is happening at the time because one is thinking of something else.

The teacher scolded the young boy for *daydreaming* during the math lesson.

deal with (v) To handle a person or situation.

I had to *deal with* an angry teenager when I said she couldn't go to the rock concert.

deodorant (n) A product used under the arms to prevent body odor.

Using a *deodorant* is especially important during hot weather.

devil's advocate (n) One who takes the opposite side in an argument to bring out all points that need to be discussed.

Although he agreed with the Equal Rights Amendment, he played *devil's advocate* by pretending to be against it while asking good questions.

dial (v) To select the numbers on the telephone.

How do you *dial* a long-distance call?

discount (n) A reduction in price.

The store was offering a 10 percent *discount* on all children's clothes.

dressy (adj) Fancy or special (clothes).

Do you think this outfit is *dressy* enough for a wedding?

farmer's market (n) A place where farmers sell their fresh fruits, vegetables, and meats to the public. (Also called *public market*.)

It's much cheaper to buy food at the local *farmer's market* than in a supermarket.

fast food (n) Food such as hamburgers and hot dogs that is available without waiting.

If we eat *fast food*, we can finish lunch quickly and have more time to shop.

feel free (v) To be comfortable enough in someone's company to do or to say what is on your mind.

When I am at my friend's house, I *feel free* to take a drink from the refrigerator.

first impression (n) The feeling that one has about a person when meeting or seeing the person for the first time.

My *first impression* of him was very different from the way I feel about him now; at first I thought he was uncaring, but now I know that he's shy.

fix someone up (v) To arrange a date for a friend.

Mary offered *to fix Jane up* with a date while she was visiting her in Chicago.

forward (v) To send mail to another address.

The post office will *forward* your mail to your new address if you ask them to.

fun-loving (adj) Enjoying having a good time.

Marty is a *fun-loving* person; she knows how to amuse herself and those around her.

go ahead (v) To begin; to proceed.

When my mother got on the line, the operator told me to *go ahead*.

go out (v) To date.

Will you *go out* with me Saturday night?

groom (n) A man who is getting married.

The *groom* looked very nervous before the wedding ceremony.

hair spray (n) A liquid that is sprayed on the hair to keep it in place.

Most hairstylists use *hair spray* on their customers' hair to keep it in place.

hairstyle (n) The way in which a person wears his or her hair.

Some women look better in long *hairstyles*, which seem softer and more romantic.

handsome (adj) Nice-looking (usually refers to a male).

I think he is *handsome* because he has beautiful eyes and dark hair.

hardware store (n) A store that sells tools, paint, pipes, nails, and other equipment needed to make general repairs or alterations on a building.

We bought some insulation, a hammer, a screwdriver, and a ladder at the *hardware store*.

hold one's own (v) To assert oneself; to take an active part.

Although she was hesitant about speaking in public, she managed to *hold her own* quite nicely.

home remedies (n) Cures or purported cures that people pass from generation to generation.

Chicken soup is a *home remedy* for a cold, the flu, or an upset stomach.

homesick (adj) Feeling sad about being separated from one's home and family.

He was *homesick* as soon as the plane left the airport.

honeymoon (n) The vacation a newly married couple takes after the wedding.

Niagara Falls is a popular spot for people to go on their *honeymoon*.

house call (n) A visit made by a doctor to the home of a sick person.

Doctors used to make *house calls;* nowadays, patients must come to the doctor's office or to the emergency room at the hospital for treatment.

hygiene (n) Care and cleanliness of the body.

Good *hygiene* will not only keep you clean but will also help you stay healthy.

image (n) The way something looks; appearance.

The *image* of a very tall, thin, muscular man makes me think of a basketball player.

intention (n) What someone plans to do.

Was it your *intention* to make me angry by ignoring me?

intimate (adj) Very personal.

I had an *intimate* discussion with my best friend about my personal problems.

landlord (n) A property owner who rents apartments, houses, or office space to others.

George called the *landlord* to have him fix the leaky water pipes.

lasagna (n) A popular Italian dish consisting of layers of wide noodles, cheese, meat, and tomato sauce.

Lasagna is one of my favorite foods, even though it's fattening.

lay (someone) off (v) To cease to employ someone, usually temporarily.

Because the company had lost much business, it *laid off* a dozen workers.

love life (n) The romance in one's life.

Most people consider the details of their *love life* to be confidential; they talk about them only with intimate friends.

makeup (n) Cosmetics that women use to improve their appearance, such as lipstick, powder, and mascara.

Most women look more attractive with a little *makeup*.

make up (v) To apologize and become friends again after having quarreled.

Jim and Sally *make up* each time they have a fight by remembering how much they love each other.

match (v) To put together two or more items that are similar.

Sometimes it is very hard to find a blouse to *match* a skirt.

mayonnaise (n) A sauce made of eggs, vinegar, and oil and used on sandwiches and in salads.

When I told the waitress that I didn't want *mayonnaise* on my sandwich, she yelled to the kitchen, "Hold the mayo!"

medicated (adj) A product that contains some form of medicine.

She uses a specially *medicated* cream to cure her baby's diaper rash.

mutual (adj) Common to both.

After we talked and compared notes, we found that we had several *mutual* friends and *mutual* interests.

nonverbal (adj) Without words.

A smile is a pleasant form of *nonverbal* communication.

Odor Eaters (n) Brand name for a product used to absorb unpleasant odors in the shoes.

He bought *Odor Eaters* for his shoes when he noticed that they smelled bad.

opposite sex (n) The sex other than one's own.

Shy people often have trouble talking with members of the *opposite sex*.

out front (adv) In front of a building.

I'll meet you *out front* in ten minutes.

overall (adv) Generally.

Although I have complaints about the food, *overall* I would rate the vacation as outstanding.

pair up (v) To form pairs, especially opposite-sex pairs who spend much time together.

In high school, boys and girls often *pair up*.

patient (n) Someone who is under the care of a doctor or dentist.

Five *patients* were waiting to see the doctor.

patient (adj) Not in a hurry.

Be *patient*. Someone will assist you shortly.

perception (n) The way one sees things.

Our *perception* of life changes as we get older.

personal questions (n) Questions about things that people do not want to share, such as their income, age, or weight.

Unless you are a very close friend, you should not ask *personal questions* about anyone.

physician (n) Doctor.

What *physician* do you use?

positive (adj) In medicine, a term indicating that the bacterium or virus tested for has been found.

The throat culture is *positive*. You will have to take penicillin for ten days.

posture (n) The way one holds one's body when standing or sitting.

People who stand up straight have good *posture*.

privacy (n) Not being disturbed, staying to oneself.

I enjoy socializing, but I also enjoy the *privacy* of my room. There I can be alone with my thoughts, my music, and my books.

profile (n) Side view of a person's face.

Tom drew a lovely *profile* of Dottie's face.

pushy (adj) Trying to get others to do things they either are not ready to do or don't want to do.

Valerie is well liked because she compromises with people; her brother is not liked because he is very *pushy*.

raffle (n) A money-raising event where chances are sold to win a certain item.

The prize for the *raffle* was a 24-inch color television.

rain check (n) A credit from a store to buy a particular out-of-stock product on another day.

You may use this *rain check* next week when our new supply of Aunt Rhona's chocolate cake comes in.

receipt (n) A paper that shows that you have paid for a product or service.

Because I didn't have the *receipt* to prove that I had bought the shirt in that store, I couldn't return it.

receiving line (n) A line formed by people being honored at a reception. Guests walk from one honored person to another, congratulating them.

Of the people on the *receiving line*, we knew only the bride and groom.

reception (n) A party held after an event such as a marriage ceremony.

The wedding *reception* was held at a lovely restaurant.

rest room (n) Public toilet.

Can you tell me where the *rest room* is?

seconds (n) A portion of food offered after the first serving.

Although he was still hungry, he was too shy to ask for *seconds*.

See you later. (v) Good-bye.

I have to go now. *See you later*.

service (n) Religious ritual performed at a wedding or funeral.
  We attended the funeral *service* at the chapel.

shake (n) A drink made of ice cream, whipped cream, flavored sauce, and milk, beaten to a frothy consistency. (Also called *milkshake*.)
  A strawberry *shake* is refreshing on a hot day.

shrug (v) To lift and drop one's shoulders.
  He *shrugged* to indicate that he didn't know the answer.

side effects (n) Complications or problems.
  The *side effects* of this drug are sleepiness and dizziness.

singles bar (n) A bar where unmarried people go to meet each other.
  Joan met her husband at a *singles bar*.

stock (n) The inventory or goods a storekeeper has on the premises.
  We don't have that item in *stock*.

strep throat (n) Illness caused by the streptococcus bacterium.
  She was absent from school for three days with a *strep throat*.

stuffed shells (n) Large macaroni shaped like shells, filled with cheese and cooked in tomato sauce.
  The *stuffed shells* were very tasty.

superstition (n) A belief in something that is illogical or scientifically untrue.
  In the United States, people have *superstitions* that the number 13 is unlucky and that breaking a mirror brings bad luck.

to go (adv) An idiom used in a fast-food or other restaurant indicating that you will not eat the food in the restaurant but will take it with you to eat it elsewhere.
  Give me a cheeseburger, ketchup only, a large order of french fries, and a strawberry shake *to go*.

upset (adj) Feeling uneasy or emotionally uncomfortable.
  When I failed history I was very *upset*.

vet (n) Short for *veterinarian*. A doctor who treats animals.
  I took my dog to the *vet* for his shots.

white lie (n) A falsehood told to avoid hurting someone's feelings or to keep one from getting into trouble.
  She didn't want to go out with him, so she told a *white lie:* She said she had another date.

wink (v) To close and quickly open one eye.
  Uncle Tom smiled and *winked* at Mary as he gave her some candy.

you're kidding An expression to mean someone is joking, or that you don't believe what someone has told you.
  When Robert told his sister that he had broken his arm she said, *"you're kidding!"*